THE ACTS OF JOHN

Early Christian Apocrypha

Julian V. Hills

Harold W. Attridge

Dennis R. MacDonald

VOLUME 1: THE ACTS OF ANDREW
VOLUME 2: THE EPISTLE OF THE APOSTLES
VOLUME 3: THE ACTS OF THOMAS
VOLUME 4: THE ACTS OF PETER
VOLUME 5: DIDACHE
VOLUME 6: THE ACTS OF JOHN

THE ACTS OF JOHN

Richard I. Pervo

With Julian V. Hills

POLEBRIDGE PRESS
Salem, Oregon

Copyright © 2016 by Richard Pervo

All rights reserved. Printed in the United States of America. No part of this book may be used or reproduced in any manner whatsoever without written permission except in the case of brief quotations embodied in critical articles and reviews. For information address Polebridge Press, Willamette University, 900 State Street, Salem, OR 97301.

Cover and interior design by Robaire Ream

Library of Congress Cataloging-in-Publication Data

Pervo, Richard I.
  The Acts of John / by Richard I. Pervo with Julian V. Hills.
    pages cm. -- (Early Christian apocrypha ; volume 6)
  Includes bibliographical references and index.
  ISBN 978-1-59815-167-1 (alk. paper)
  1. Acts of John--Criticism, interpretation, etc. I. Hills, Julian Victor. II. Title.
  BS2880.J62P67 2016
  229'.925--dc23

                                                2015017538

CONTENTS

Preface	ix
Sigla	x
Introduction	1
The Acts of John	27
From Ephesus to Miletus (18–36)	28
A Deutero-Johannine "Book of Glory" (87–105)	38
The Fall of the House of Artemis (37–55)	49
Antipatros Recovers His Sons (56–57)	57
From Laodicea to Ephesus for a Second Visit (58–62)	59
Drusiana and Kallimachos (63–86)	61
The Farewell and Death of John (106–115)	72
Appendices	79
Bibliography	89
Index of Ancient Sources	95

SERIES PREFACE

The series *Early Christian Apocrypha & (ECA&)*, the first such publication by North American scholars, is designed as a study edition of early Christian apocryphal texts and related writings. These comprise the standard set of New Testament apocrypha (gospels, acts, epistles, apocalypses) along with other, some less well known, writings that emerged from the early Christian movement, such as homiletical, polemical, exegetical, and church order tracts. Writings reckoned "orthodox" and "heretical" by contemporaries and later authorities will be included.

The publisher and the editors have had several goals in mind. First, to provide quotable and lively renderings into modern U.S. English—satisfying both to the specialist and to the non-expert reader. Second, to offer full introductions and bibliographies that will situate the texts in question in their larger Christian and Greco-Roman contexts. Third, to supply brief commentary explaining technical aspects of the writing and the movement of the text—storyline or theological argument. Fourth, to add "verse numbers" where previous editions gave only larger section or chapter numbers.

Where appropriate, the texts will be annotated with cross-references, not only within the biblical canon but also outside it—in due course supplying a network of interconnected references to assist comparative study. A full index of texts, biblical and non-biblical, will conclude each volume.

PREFACE

Julian V. Hills carefully reviewed the translation with his skilled and prudent eye. He also supplied the "verse" numbers as well as contributing many of the notes and references. Thanks are due to István Czachez, Trevor Thompson, Julia Snyder, and to the staff of Polebridge Press.

—Richard Pervo

SIGLA, ABBREVIATIONS, CONVENTIONS

Aaa	Lipsius-Bonnet, *Acta apostolorum apocrypha*
ApocActs	Apocryphal Acts of Apostles
AAn	*The Acts of Andrew*
AAnMt	*The Acts of Andrew and Matthias*
AAnPas	The final (Passion Narrative) section of *The Acts of Andrew*
AJn	*The Acts of John*
APl	*The Acts of Paul*
APt	*The Acts of Peter*
APtBG	*The Act of Peter*
ATh	*The Acts of Thomas*
ANF	Roberts-Donaldson, *Ante-Nicene Fathers*
Bonnet	The *Aaa* edition of AJn, prepared by Maximilian Bonnet
CANT	Geerard, *Clavis*
Ep apost	*Epistle of the Apostles*
GPet	*Gospel of Peter*
H	Codex Halki, Mon. Trin. 102, an important eleventh-century manuscript of AJn
Junod-Kaestli	Junod and Kaestli, *Acta Iohannis*
LPGL	Lampe, *Patristic Greek Lexicon*
LSJ	Liddell Scott Jones, *Greek-English Lexicon*
NHC	Nag Hammadi Codex
*NTApoc*²	Schneemelcher, *New Testament Apocrypha*
P. Oxy.	Oxyrhynchus Papyri
Schäferdiek	Trans. of *Acts of John* in *NTApoc*
v.l.	*varia lectio*, an alternate reading found in one or more witnesses.
<and>	partial and somewhat conjectural restoration
[then]	words not in the original supplied for clarity or continuity
italics	phrases suspected as secondary additions or substitutions
. . .	a lacuna (gap) in the text
►	indicates the place where the principal reference list of passages related by a common theme or expression is to be found

x

INTRODUCTION

THE TEXT OF
THE ACTS OF JOHN[1]

Note: The *Acts of John* (AJn) rests upon a thin and incomplete basis. This is not unusual, not only for Christian apocrypha, but also for many ancient texts. Those trained in biblical studies learn to prefer shorter texts, as copyists and editors tended to clarify and correct through supplementation. With regard to narrative, such as hagiography (saints' lives), the opposite tendency also applied. Texts were shortened for a variety of reasons, including theology and practicality.

Two sixteenth-century manuscripts, R and Z,[2] have long constituted the basis of editions.[3] Two others M (twelfth-thirteenth century) and O (tenth) offer a less complete but often better text. Junod and Kaestli were able to make use of the eleventh-century palimpsest H (Halki 102), which, where legible and available, often has a superior text.[4] These manuscripts attest to chapters 18–55, 58–86, and 106–15, the major narrative components of AJn. The last of these, called the Metastasis ("change of place," a term also used for the Assumption of the Virgin), exists in three editions in twenty manuscripts.[5] Since Junod and Kaestli some fragments of chapters 63–86 and 106–15 have

---

1. For a thorough discussion of data available up to the date of publication see Junod-Kaestli, 1:1–63. Lallemann, *Acts of John,* has a concise summary: 6–14, the sources of these statements.
2. When an approximate date is assigned to a MS, the basis is usually the style of the handwriting. Specific dates reflect a colophon, in which the scribe usefully notes the exact date of completion.
3. The associated K is a copy of R.
4. A palimpsest is a parchment text that was erased to provide opportunity for a fresh text. By various means scholars attempt to recover the underlying, erased work(s).
5. In all of the ApocActs the final chapter is multiply attested because of its liturgical use, on the feast of the apostle. These scenes were also highly and frequently edited.

been published.⁶ The last two items indicate that the late medieval text of AJn has been abbreviated.

Several witnesses contain but a portion of AJn. C (1319 CE) is the sole witness to the "embedded gospel" of chapters 87–105. The eleventh-century Q has the story of John and the partridge, numbered chapters 56–57 in the edition of Bonnet. Junod-Kaestli exclude this episode from the ancient AJn.⁷ Under those numbers they include a story set in Smyrna, found in two manuscripts, L and S, of the tenth and eleventh centuries.⁸

The story of the portrait of John (chapters 26–29) was not a prescient inclusion by the author, as its rejection of the value of images endeared it to iconoclasts, leading to the condemnation of AJn by the last Ecumenical Council (Nicea II, 787).⁹ On the positive side the Acts of the Council cites parts of chapters 27–28, 93–95, and 97–98. These citations show that the AJn was a unified work and that the embedded gospel was a part of it. None can claim that AJn is a modern construct.¹⁰

The text lacks integrity, an ideal example of which would be a complete, unedited copy of the original. The beginning is lost; other gaps (lacunae) may be identified or posited, and some interpolations have been made. The largest generally accepted interpolations are chapters 94–102 and 109.¹¹

Censorship also played a role.¹² In the case of AJn scenes portraying wives in successful rebellion against their husbands have been obliterated,¹³ as well as the exhortation to celibacy at a wedding reception.¹⁴ Orthodox Christianity held that celibacy was for the religious and that wives were to obey their husbands. Theological condemnation was also rigorous. Since icono-

---

6. See Jenkins, "Papyrus 1" and Gardner and Worp, "Leaves."

7. Junod-Kaestli, 1:145–53. Lallemann, *Acts of John*, leaves the question "open," permitting him to use the episode in his investigation. Janet Spittler offers no explicit judgment, but gives arguments supporting exclusion of this episode, *Animals*, 116–25.

8. Possible fragments of AJn are treated in Appendix A.

9. Junod-Kaestli, 1:344–68.

10. This argument has been made regarding the APl, in an able argument (with which I do not agree) by Snyder, *Acts of Paul*.

11. Czachesz ("Eroticism," 71–72) suggests that John's speeches in AJn 88–105 and 113–14 were probably added c. 200.

12. Lalleman, *Acts of John*, 22–23, is skeptical about censorship, but the evidence cited in the following notes is difficult to refute.

13. Similar scenes are known from other acts. Junod-Kaestli, 1.105 n.1, show how slender the manuscript tradition for these episodes in the several apocryphal acts actually is.

14. See Appendix A.2.

Introduction 3

clasts found aid and comfort in chapters 25–29, their victorious opponents condemned it. Except for the fortuitous preparation and survival of a single manuscript, the contents of chapters 87–105 would have left no more than traces of their anathematization.[15]

The task of recovering/reconstructing the ancient AJn is especially difficult. Researchers must identify and extract earlier traditions from certain manuscripts of the later editions in which they are usually embedded, establish from these a critical text, determine the probable ancient order of the passages, identify apparent gaps in the reconstructed text as well as their possible contents, and then isolate possible layers of tradition within the ancient material, taking into account the probability that varying editions already existed in antiquity. In addition there are several fragments that must be related to extant sections of the AJn or hypothetically assigned to gaps in the witnesses, and a number of ancient stories about John requiring evaluation of their possible relevance. The ultimate result should seek to present a picture of an apparently coherent underlying structure of the text.

The following sections of the ancient Acts, most of which have distinct textual attestations and histories, have been identified:

A. Chapters 18–55[16]
B. Chapters 58–86
C. Chapters 106–15
D. Chapters 56–57
E. Chapters 87–105

According to the oft-cited *Stichometry* included within the writings of Nicephorus,[17] about 68% of AJn survives.[18] This figure would approximate the size of Matthew. (Stichometry was a technique developed in the early Hellenistic period to classify books by their size, computed by the number of standardized lines. This would help copyists determine what could fit upon the available space and also signal accidental or intentional abridgements. Unfortunately, the standardized length of a line varied, so the data provide only approximate

---

15. See the references to the Acts by the Second Council of Nicaea and by Augustine *Ep.* 237, in Junod-Kaestli, 1:26, and their summary comments on the transmission of the text, 1:101–6.

16. Recent translators and editors omit chs. 1–17 of Bonnet's edition as obviously secondary. (Bonnet did not claim that this material was original.) Bernard Pick (*The Apocryphal Acts*, 126–35) provides a translation. See Appendix C.

17. 758–826, Patriarch of Constantinople. The stichometric data were added to Nicephorus' writings. They are probably roughly contemporary with him.

18. See Junod-Kaestli, *L'histoire,* 126–29.

limits.)[19] Junod and Kaestli (*Acta Johannis*, 1:106) believe that AJn was longer than the Nicephorean data suggest. Certainty is elusive.[20]

Blocks ABC are clearly sequential, but the beginning is missing and there is a gap between A and B. The location of D and E must be determined by investigation. As is true for all but the ATh among the major ApocActs, the opening is lost. Proposals about its contents may reveal more about the views of particular scholars than about AJn, but the question merits attention.[21] A guiding assumption is that John the son of Zebedee worked in/was assigned the province of Asia.[22] In so far as one can tell from the text, he is the first to proclaim the gospel in Ephesus. This has important ramifications for the work's viewpoint, for it thoroughly ignores any trace of Pauline missionary activity there. (See below.) A mission in Miletus may be assumed, as John has already gathered some followers and traveling companions.

(*Lacuna i*) One possible opening is an account of the Apostolic Lottery in Jerusalem, at which John was awarded Asia.[23] En route he may have been shipwrecked, a perfectly proper apostolic credential. The Syriac history of John reports the equivalent of a lottery.[24] Prochorus reports the assignment of lots and a shipwreck. In the secondary text of AJn *in Rome* printed by Bonnet one can observe both additional circumstantial detail and an effort to link all the components of the tradition.[25] Outside of travel from Palestine to Asia Minor, which had to be accomplished by some means, the tradition is uniform about Miletus and Ephesus as the initial stations. This could weaken a second option: that AJn began with John's release from Patmos,[26] if one hypothesizes that the beginning was suppressed rather than lost by accident.[27] Nothing in this scenario would stimulate suppression. A difficulty with proposing a damaged manuscript is that the damage would have had to affect the entire tradition, as all of the secondary works cohere where chapter 18 begins. One point in favor of this hypothesis is that John is characterized as

---

19. Turner, *Greek Manuscripts*, 19.
20. Not only is line length uncertain but the scope of the edition used for this calculation is unknown. It might have been longer or shorter than the original
21. See Junod-Kaestli, 1:81–86 and those cited subsequently here.
22. That province included the western portion of present-day Turkey.
23. This lottery is inspired by Acts 1:15–26, but quite different in result. The lottery is reported at the beginning of ATh and the *Acts of Andrew and Matthias*. See Kaestli, "Scènes d'attribution."
24. Wright, *Apocryphal Acts*, 2:5, somewhat modulated. On this text see Appendix C.
25. Bonnet II.1.159–60. (This variant is not included in the detailed work on this text by Junod-Kaestli, 2:835–66.)
26. Lalleman, *Acts of John*, 15–16; Czachesz, *Commission Narratives*, 93–97.
27. MSS are more vulnerable at the beginning and end.

Introduction 5

"elderly" in the painting (chapter 28).[28] A difficulty is that no one in Ephesus or Smyrna—the cities addressed in Revelation 2–3 identified here—has embraced the Christian message.[29]

Yet another option looks to the apostle's closing words in chapter 113, which summarize appearances of the Risen One exhorting John not to marry. They reflect a commission account, highly appropriate for the opening of an Acts.[30] This scene appears to be echoed in the Pseudo-Titus material (Appendix A.2). Evidence in support of a narration of that call to celibacy and mission comes from the illustrated life of John, which depict him abandoning a woman and taking refuge in the lap of Jesus.[31]

If the AJn included such an initial commission, complete with blinding as a punishment, it would parallel the story of Paul's commission (Acts 9; 22; 26) and the hypothetical opening of APl, which the author of AJn quite probably knew. APl evidently repeats the story of the apostle's commission in chapter 9. From a literary perspective this would form a fine bracket (*inclusio*) about the AJn, a fond and common device. For structural, literary, and secondary evidential reasons this proposal is appealing. Also in its favor are plausible reasons for its eventual suppression: The break-up of lawful engagements or marriages by believers was not generally favored, the story vaunts the superiority of a single apostle, and it may be read as an endorsement of same-sex relationships.[32]

(*Lacuna ii*) A gap appears at the close of 36, which the manuscript tradition has elided with a brief summary. In all probability the healing of aged women in the Temple of Artemis was followed by a report of Drusiana's conversion and subsequent alienation from her husband following her withdrawal from the conjugal bed. Her then unbelieving spouse, Andronikos, had locked her in a tomb to die and threw in the apostle John for good measure. Since Andronikos appears in chapter 31 as an opponent of John, the tale probably began there. Supporting data may be found in two indirect sources: The *Manichaean Psalm-Book* reports: "John the Virgin, he also was made to drink the cup/fourteen days imprisoned that he might die of hunger" (142:23–24), and "… that loves [her] master is Drusiane, the lover of God, shut [up for fourteen] days,

---

28. Noted by Lalleman, *Acts of John*, 16. See however, AJn 28.6.
29. Although this might not have troubled later readers, it is difficult to imagine that it escaped the notice of the author.
30. Czachesz, *Commission Narratives*, 111–15.
31. Cartlidge, "Evangelist."
32. In various publications Czachesz has stressed kinship with the Platonic tradition (especially the *Symposium*) and its analogical and metaphoric use of erotic language.

questioning her apostle" (192:32–193:1). These Coptic texts witness to a tradition that the two were imprisoned together. The second of these references is part of a catalogue of heroines of the apocryphal acts.[33] The other datum is the depiction of the baptism of Drusiana.[34] The episode was probably suppressed because it portrayed a lawfully married woman rebelling against her husband's claim of conjugal rights.[35]

Knut Schäferdiek offered strong arguments for the relocation of the chapters numbered 87–105 (which occur in a manuscript without context) by Bonnet, who had assumed that the beginning of chapter 87 referred to an appearance of the Lord to Drusiana after her death, an appearance occasioned by her guilt at being an object of lust.[36] Pieter Lalleman has proposed to return to Bonnet's arrangement of 87–105.[37] His argument is grounded in a distaste for proposals about lost incidents. Since chapter 82 does refer to the former conflict between Drusiana and Andronikos, the data cited above portrays that very incident, and Byzantine critics tended to remove such scenes, Schäferdiek's reconstruction is more cogent.

(*Lacuna iii*) Between chapters 105 and 37 there is another lacuna, as the former lacks narrative closure. The extent and contents are unknown.[38]

(*Lacunae iv–v*) Chapters 37–55 form an *inclusio* inspired by Acts 19:21–20:1: a new journey is announced, followed by an incident in the Ephesian theater, after which the journey is launched. Since a transition between chapters 55 and 58 is lacking, Junod and Kaestli insert the Smyrna episode which they number chapters 56–57 here.[39] This does not, however, fill in the gap, for the subheading introduced in manuscripts at 58 reveals that, at the very least, episodes from Laodicea are missing. Visits to other cities cannot be ruled out. One proposal looks to the seven cities of Revelation.[40] More recently, Eckhard Plümacher has proposed the provincial governor's judicial circuit.[41] A more important and at present unsolvable problem is the extent of this journey in the narrative. The length of this journey is difficult to estimate. Ephesus was the central site of AJn; for later editors it became essentially the only site.

In outline form the hypothetically reconstructed AJn may be outlined as follows. (This is not an attempt to provide a literary plan of the book.)

---

33. Page and line references are from Allberry, *Manichaean Psalm-Book*.
34. Cartlidge and Elliott, *Art,* fig 6.5, p. 190.
35. For a detailed argument see Junod-Kaestli, 1:86–90.
36. Schäferdiek, "Acts of John," 2:178–79.
37. Lalleman, *Acts of John*, 25–27. Klauck, "Acts of John," 22, leaves the question open.
38. Junod-Kaestli, 1:91–92.
39. Junod-Kaestli, 1:91–92.
40. Lalleman, *Acts of John*, 25–27; Junod-Kaestli, 1:93–94.
41. Plümacher, "Apostolische Missionsreise."

Introduction

1. *Lacuna i: Opening of work, Palestine (or Patmos) to Miletus, the length is unknown*
2. Chapters 18–36 (A): Miletus to Ephesus, Lykomedes and Kleopatra, preparation for mass healing in the theater
3. *Lacuna ii: Healings, conversion of Drusiana, imprisonment, release/rescue, conversion of Andronikos*
4. Chapters 87–105 (less 94–102) (E): "A Deutero-Johannine Book of Glory"
5. *Lacuna iii: Contents unknown*
6. Chapters 37–55 (A): The fall of the Temple of Artemis and its aftermath, the story of a young adulterer, and plans to evangelize Smyrna
7. *Lacuna iv: Preparations for and progress of a journey to Smyrna (and probably additional material)*
8. Chapters 56–57 (D): Antipater and his epileptic sons
9. *Lacuna v: Episodes in Smyrna, Laodicea and, possibly other cities*
10. Chapters 58–62 (B): Farewell to Laodicea, experiences on the road, and reception at Ephesus
11. Chapters 63–86 (B): The tale of Drusiana and Kallimachos
12. Chapters 106–115 (less 109) (C): The farewell and death of John (Metastasis)[42]

Within this framework one may attempt to locate the other fragments and attestations of lost scenes.[43]

WITNESSES TO ACTS OF JOHN

Note: Investigation of early witnesses to a text helps determine its date and place of composition, its diffusion, ancient opinions regarding its merits, popularity, and usage.

AJn benefits from a masterful monograph on the subject from the diligent and capable hands of Eric Junod and Jean-Daniel Kaestli (*L'histoire*).[44] AJn first appears on the literary radar in the last decades of the third century, at which

---

42. The basis for this outline is Junod-Kaestli, 1:98–100.
43. These texts are to be found in Appendix A to the translation. It is difficult to sustain the case for any particular placement. The fragments provide more assurance of the existence of lacunae in the tradition than of the original structure.
44. For a brief survey see Schäferdiek, "Acts of John," 152–56. As noted, medieval illustrations of the life of John provide data for filling in some of the textual gaps: Cartlidge and Elliott, *Art*, 175–77; 180–208.

time it was included in the Manichean collection of what are now called the five major apocryphal acts.[45] Until the end of the fourth century, AJn is attested as part of a group of acts.[46] The book certainly had an independent existence, but it gained no positive or negative attention from such theologians as Origen. Such neglect makes the question of date and locale more difficult to resolve. The available evidence shows no sign that AJn was viewed in late antiquity as a useful historical source—as, for example, were APt and APl—or esteemed in a particular region, as was ATh.

Ancient versions of ApocActs serve several purposes, including witnesses of texts lost in the original, examples of an earlier form of the earliest text, and evidence for the diffusion and popularity of the works. With the standard exception of the Metastasis (final scene), none of the ancient Johannine narratives, other than a part of the Latin *Virtutes Iohannis* (Miracles of John), exhibit much if any influence from the AJn.[47] Editors typically focused on wonders, reduced or eliminated speeches, and scrubbed ApocActs of such unorthodox elements as they could detect. By comparison with the other ApocActs, AJn was all bath water.

LITERARY GENRE AND CHARACTER; STYLE AND TECHNIQUE

Note: Generic classification is not a matter of providing useful labels. Genre indicates where a book would be lodged on the shelves, what it is like, and what expectations readers might have. Ancient generic categories are interesting, but contemporary critics use terms that communicate today.

---

45. The Manichean movement was an adaptable world religion that extended from Spain to China. It was a book religion that utilized the sacred writings of many cults in the service of its mission.

46. Manichean psalms: Allberry, *Manichaean Psalm-Book*, 192–93. The Greek east: Eusebius, *Ecclesiastical History* 3.25.6; Epiphanius, *Panarion*, 47.1 (c. 375). The Latin west: The Priscillianists. (Priscillian led a strongly ascetic renewal movement in what is now Spain and southern France. Heretical features of his teaching are scarce; the group did read apocryphal texts, probably disseminated by Manicheans.) Epiphanius may also refer to a specific passage from AJn (*Panarion* 79.5). Thereafter comes a thin trickle of possible and probable references. Photius (third or fourth quarter of ninth century) knows the ApocActs as a book (Codex 114), although his comments focus upon AJn.

47. On traditions in various languages see Junod-Kaestli, 1:40–44. "Ancient" is important. The medieval West shows evidence of use of the AJn. See "Reception," below.

Introduction

The various ApocActs have long been viewed as a group, and for good reason. Each relates the career of an early Christian missionary. Because they do not describe in any detail ancestry, infancy, and childhood, they are not biographies. The pattern for all of the Acts is provided, or modeled, by the Gospel of Mark, which opens with the outset of Jesus' career and ends with his death and an announcement that he belongs to another realm. Canonical Acts resembles Mark, with its beginning in call and mission and abrupt ending. The successive Acts tend to end less abruptly, but the pattern is similar.[48] Formally, if not excessively informatively, such works are monographs. Surviving classical examples are Latin and known by the name of their primary subject.[49] The title *Praxeis* ("Acts"), with its connotation of outstanding deeds by major figures, while not original to the canonical book, is appropriate for all.[50] AJn is an historical monograph in form; its content is fictional. No good arguments can be made for the use of traditions other than the identification of John the son of Zebedee with a Christian active in Ephesus.[51] This is a work of fiction composed by its author. It is therefore a kind of historical novel.[52]

Ancient fiction influenced the Acts in various ways. Comparison of these texts with popular fiction shows that one object of the Acts was to entertain. Sometimes this involves competition with "pagan" novels, but it is equally clear that Christian authors wished to engage their audiences' attention rather than simply to give them fiction of a more edifying quality.[53]

The development of the apocryphal tradition shows a gradual mastery over and transcendence of limits imposed by the brief units derived from oral tradition; that is, the constituent forms found in the Synoptic Gospels: sayings, anecdotes, parables, brief accounts of healings and exorcisms. The various acts are the best surviving examples of this process, already visible in

---

48. Only in ATh does an apocryphal acts preserve the beginning.

49. Sallust: wars with Jugurtha and Catiline; Tacitus: *Agricola*.

50. On the title see R. Pervo, *Acts*, 29–30. ("Acts of the Apostles" is clearly secondary. The major character, Paul, is not an apostle in Acts; Peter is the sole apostle to receive attention.) In order to distinguish canonical from apocryphal books church authorities came to label ApocActs as "Journeys (*periodoi*) of Paul," etc.

51. One can, however, argue that AJn exhibits some knowledge about Ephesus: Engelmann, "Ephesos." The standard argument against local knowledge is Schäferdiek, "Herkunft."

52. Junod and Kaestli prefer to see the work as an original creation that cannot be assigned to a single genre, "Actes de Jean," 982. "Sui generis" arguments tend to be useful half-truths: every work is somewhat unique; a completely unique piece would be unintelligible.

53. Specific argument has been advanced for the influence of *Callirhoe*, an early romantic novel, upon AJn: Junod-Kaestli, 2:516–20; Lalleman, *Acts of John*, 148–49.

the differences between Acts and Luke. From a literary viewpoint the Christian apocrypha often reveal improvement upon, rather than decline from, the NT.

Like the canonical Acts, AJn (and other ApocActs) prefer speeches cast into recognizable rhetorical form (for example, 20, 33–36, 39–40, 67–69)[54] to the stringing together of various sayings, and the development of complex and interwoven narrative episodes to narrative miniatures. Prayers (for example, 22, 41, 108) are often lengthy.[55] Healings, revivals of the dead and exorcisms (chapters 36, 23, and 57, respectively) are not lacking. Chapters 60–61 is an extensive Pronouncement Story.[56] Resurrections are the dominant type of miracle. Although symbolism is arguably present already in the canonical gospel miracles, in AJn it is patent and prevalent.

The preferred narrative technique is a series of often interlinked *novelle* that incorporate discourses.[57] The best example from AJn is the story of Drusiana and Kallimachos (chapters 63–86), which reveals no little skill in plotting and arrangement.[58] Despite the number of minor characters, Drusiana and Kallimachos remain at the center of the action, from which the figure of John is never distant. The author has integrated what seem to be most of the motifs of ancient popular fiction into a cohesive literary unity that evokes every emotion and never wants for excitement—which is not to say taste. This story of Drusiana is the leading candidate for the author's lack of taste. That is not unintentional. Kallimachos' determination to work his will upon the deceased matron illustrates the idea that sexual intercourse is congress with a corpse. Secondarily it portrays the result of unrestrained passion. Readers of today sense a strong contrast between the content and quality of the prayers and speeches in this tale with its rather lurid narrative.

One cannot speak of a seemingly endless series of incidents linked like beads on a string until, in the last scene, the hero dies. Characters from earlier episodes reappear in later scenes. That Drusiana was twice the victim of lust, once from her husband, who imprisoned her in a tomb, and later from an outsider, whose love sickness drove her to the tomb, both unites and intensifies the plot. It also enhances the symbolic quality of the incidents.

---

54. See Pervo, "Rhetoric."

55. The Fourth Gospel, with its long speeches and prayer, as well as its proclivity toward extended narrative (e.g., John 6, 17, 11) is a precedent.

56. Pronouncement Stories or apophthegms are brief narratives with a punch line, e.g., the question of paying taxes ("Render unto Caesar"), Mark 12:13–17.

57. The Italian word *novella* does not refer to a short story but to a traditional narrative unit, such as a healing, that is expanded with often memorable circumstantial details. Examples are Mark 2:1–12 and 5:1–20.

58. On this story see Konstan, "Acts of Love."

Lykomedes has an image of John made as a consequence of his and Kleopatra's deliverance. Even chapter 30, which may at first sight seem a rough and unexpected transition, introduces an example of activities more appropriate to believers than commissioning portraits, skillfully incorporating Lykomedes and Kleopatra into this very project. Their mission in turn thrusts Andronikos onto the stage, giving occasion for the emergence of Drusiana and their (now lost) conflict.

Chapter 38 returns the action to the famous pagan temple. After the edifice has been thrown down, its former priest is raised up in a house filled with those gathered for Christian worship. There follows the tale of the reckless young adulterer (48–54), a cautionary story that brings to mind the *novelle* contained within Apuleius' *Metamorphoses*. Both of these are highly moralized, presenting, in the former incident, one who was careless of his relative's condition and, in the latter, one who murdered his father and saw castration as the solution to his libidinous urges. Contrast, parallelism, and irony are effectively deployed in this sequence, the final section of which evokes the lust of Andronikos and foreshadows that of Kallimachos.[59] The use of retardation is particularly effective. Note how the resurrection of Kleopatra is drawn out through the course of six chapters (18–23). Chapters 63–86 demonstrate skillful changes of viewpoint from one center to another, until all are brought together, without any need to resort to a "Meanwhile, back at the ranch" device. Irony governs much of the narrative, as it does in the fourth Gospel, but neither irony nor allegory dilute the vitality of the narrative. The pathos of, for example, chapters 20–21 does not suit modern taste, but antiquity held to different standards in this matter.[60]

The speeches often provide appropriate comment upon the action, not unlike the choruses of Greek tragedies. Through these discourses the author can achieve an ABA pattern, with a speech foreshadowing what will happen, the action itself, and a subsequent interpretation (for example, 38–44). The address in chapters 67–69 is an example of persuasive rhetoric of a type that could be found in philosophical discourses. Chapters 67–68 begin with a series of examples, enumerate a catalogue of vices, and finish with an inclusion reiterating the examples. Chapter 69 makes use of anaphora and antithesis. The illustration, however, comes in the following narrative, wherein Kallimachos shows how troubled souls respond to adversity. The sermon proclaims the dangers of sex and greed. The narrative illustrates these dangers in action. AJn is no artistic masterpiece, but it has literary qualities long

---

59. On the parallelism of the stories of the priest and the parricide (chs. 46–54) see J. Bolyki, "Miracle Stories," 22–25.

60. See Pervo, *Profit*, 66–69.

unappreciated. Another important constituent form is an "embedded gospel," in which the apostle narrates material from the life of Jesus: chapters 87–105.[61]

The style is florid, but not complex; that is, not composed in careful periods (the paragraph-long sentences characteristic of learned Greek prose). Common figures include, as noted, anaphora and antithesis. The author likes to heap up his expressions. Any notion worth saying once is worth saying five times. In ancient rhetorical terminology AJn is "Asianic," preferring often overwrought, emotional purple prose to the purity and clarity that marked "Atticism," a revival of fifth-century style that marked Greek composition in the first centuries of the Common Era.

INTERTEXTUALITY

Note: Identification of the sources employed in a text sheds light upon many questions, including geographical location, ideological orientation, genre, and intellectual level. Determination of who employed the work under scrutiny aids in charting its diffusion. Use of a text does not establish its authority or status *per se*. If a text reads "it is better to marry than to be aflame with passion" one may conclude that the author knows and uses 1 Cor 7:9, directly or indirectly. If the writer states "Paul says, 'It is better, …'" Paul may enjoy some authority. The statement "Holy Scripture says: 'It is better, …'" posits an authority of high standing. One should note also that "intertextuality" has become a more reflective and sophisticated discipline than traditional "source-criticism."

AJn cites no "sacred" texts (and rewrites several).[62] The chief question is: what texts does the author know and cherish? The Christian "Old Testament" is out of the picture (including Genesis 1–3, central for "Gnostics").[63] The author knew and was influenced by the canonical Acts.[64] This is evidence against the once dominant claim that canonical and apocryphal Acts are unrelated. The Synoptic Gospels are evidenced, as is also, not surprisingly, the

---

61. Other examples of this type in ApoActs are APl 13:7–11 (incomplete) and APt 20. For a discussion of this passage see below.
62. On intertextuality in AJn see Lalleman, *Acts of John*, 69–152.
63. See Karasszon, "Old Testament Quotations."
64. Karasszon, "Old Testament Quotations," 74–98; Thompson, "Claiming Ephesus." On the theory that the first person plural narration derives from Acts, however, see Snyder, "Imitation."

Introduction

Fourth Gospel.[65] Familiarity with Acts, the Synoptics, and John indicates a date no earlier than the late second century. Irenaeus (c. 180) is the first person known to have utilized all of these texts—and Paul. The last is formally absent from AJn.[66]

Both formal and thematic affinities with the *Secret Book of John*, one of the most widely disseminated "Gnostic" texts, are apparent. An intertextual link is possible.[67] (It is intriguing that, in contrast, no traces of AJn exist in the Nag Hammadi Library. A manuscript of similar character to those found at Nag Hammadi contains both the *Secret Book of John* and a selection from the APt.[68] A single papyrus fragment of AJn has been recovered thus far from Egypt.)[69] All engaged in the discussion agree that intertextual relationships occur among the ApocActs. Consensus is, however, lacking as to who borrowed from whom. The problem cannot easily be resolved without complete, early manuscripts of good quality because the texts became contaminated with one another in the course of time. (For an analogy: the text of Mark was contaminated by Matthew and Luke. Not until a good critical text of Mark was prepared did it become possible to make a convincing case that Mark was a source of Matthew and Luke.)[70] At present the most pressing question is the relation between AJn and APt. Both utilize the theme of polymorphy (the earthly Jesus, like other gods, could appear in different forms),[71] include an "embedded gospel," and do not give strong weight to apostolic travel.[72]

---

65. Snyder, "Imitation," 110–23.

66. Lalleman, *Acts of John*, 144. (See also below.)

67. Lalleman, *Acts of John*, 136–37, e.g. The links are prominent in AJn 87–105, the "embedded gospel." (Scholars tend to denominate this book as the *Apocryphon of John*.) On possible use of the *Gospel of Peter* and the *Gospel of the Savior*, see Czachesz, *Commission Narratives*, 103.

68. See Stoops, *Acts of Peter*, 13–14; 41–44.

69. P. Oxy. 850 (Appendix A). (Except for APl, Egypt has not been a rich resource of the ApocActs.)

70. See Lalleman, "Polymorphy," *Acts of John*, 99–110; Jones, "Orientations"; and the essays in Stoops, ed., *Semeia*, 80, especially those of MacDonald, Pervo, and Stoops, as found in the Bibliography. In a forthcoming essay, an advance copy of which she has kindly supplied, Julia Snyder emphasizes the shortcomings of all the approaches to intertextuality between the canonical Acts and its apocryphal successors.

71. On polymorphy see also below.

72. Stoops (*Acts of Peter*, 33–35) argues for the priority of APt, Lalleman for AJn. The case for the former is more compelling, but those who view AJn as early will not find that case convincing.

One of the more interesting examples of intertextuality is paradoxical: AJn attempts to erase the mission of Paul in Roman Asia.[73] A weak solution would be interest in establishing John with Ephesus with no attention to other Christian missionaries. Even weaker would be the hypothesis that the author of AJn was not aware of Paul's work there. Neither is cogent. AJn knows Acts. John is the first to proclaim Jesus in Ephesus.[74] According to a surface reading of Acts, Paul's mission ended in a controversy generated by partisans of Artemis (the city's patron goddess) which nearly erupted into a riot in the theater, after which Paul quietly left town.[75] These actions could be construed as far from successful and less than courageous. In AJn the apostle turns the theater into a venue for mass healing and leaves the temple of Artemis in ruins, after which he departs for further missions (chapters 30–55). John's miracles are like those of Paul.[76] On every point John may be compared with Paul and given a better grade. Coincidence is ruled out.

Replacement of Paul does not require a hostile view of Paul. In chapter 112:1 John prays: "You who have chosen us for a mission to the Gentiles, God, ..." appropriating both Paul's title and language.[77] Replacement thereby acquires an undeniable edge. As Thompson indicates, AJn and Paul—both the letter-writing apostle and the speech-making non-apostle—do not have similar views about Jesus' death and resurrection.[78] AJn belongs in the column labeled "anti-Pauline."

ORIGINAL AUDIENCE, LOCALE, AND DATE

Note: Pursuit of answers to the journalistic questions: To whom, When, Where should be of obvious importance to understanding, for solutions to these will illuminate the issues and concerns motivating an author. The goal of criticism is to provide a coherent and cohesive picture in which the components mutually reinforce one another. Consider a fully furnished dining room of a wealthy seventeenth-century Dutch

---

73. Credit for exposing this belongs to Trevor Thompson, "Claiming Ephesus."
74. To be precise, neither Acts nor scholarship claim priority for Paul there, but Ephesus was a major center of his mission.
75. In APl 9 the apostle does speak in the theater, is rescued from death at the hands of wild beasts by a miracle or two, and leaves town in the wake of the resultant chaos.
76. Lalleman, *Acts of John*, 19
77. ἐκλεξάμενος ἡμᾶς εἰς ἀποστολὴν ἐθνῶν, lit. "Having chosen me for an apostolate to the gentiles." This closely resembles Gal 2:8. (Even if the chapter has been subject to later editing, these words are unlikely to have been subsequent additions.)
78. Thompson, "Claiming Ephesus," 396–400.

merchant. Books like AJn are like many houses, with different pieces introduced at different times and some redecoration. The critic, like a television antiques appraiser, will note what has been added, removed, or altered over time. The "original" is an hypothesis. That is inevitable. ("Mere hypothesis" amounts to "an hypothesis I don't like.")

Although AJn could presumably be read by non-believers as a means for arousing interest, its primary purpose was probably to uphold the faith of a particular group, or groups, of Christians. It may have been written in the light of pressures to adhere to forms of the faith more willing to compromise with the world. In so far as this is propaganda, it is more likely a reinforcement and stimulus to insiders than a text designed for missionary purposes.[79] In general conformity with the Johannine tradition, the original audience was probably small, at least in their self-conception, and rather isolated—what is conventionally called "sectarian." In support of this is the absence of testimonies about the book until it becomes part of a collection.

That lack of circulation and discussion complicates questions about its date and place of origin. Estimates of the former range over nearly a century.[80] Candidates for the latter include Egypt, Syria, and Asia Minor.[81] The most likely places of origin are Asia Minor, Egypt, and Greek-speaking Syria. The first has in its favor the setting of the work. Against it is the absence of any firm local tradition. Junod-Kaestli support Egypt with linguistic arguments that are variously received. Egypt would be a suitable place for revision of the text—as would Syria. The "Johannine traditions" show movement from Syria to Ephesus. This does not demand a complete migration; Asia Minor, long excluded on the ground of absence of knowledge about Ephesus, has been proposed again by Lalleman, who suggests Smyrna.

An important factor is AJn's patent effort to eradicate any traces of Paul from the Ephesian tradition.[82] That intimates not only a desire to promote a

---

79. J. Snyder, "Imitation" (forthcoming) validly criticizes the claim that AJn sought to evangelize outsiders.

80. 125–50 CE (Lalleman, *Acts of John*, 268–70); first quarter of third century (Junod-Kaestli, 2:694–700). Others: Bremmer ("Women," 54-56), second century; Klauck, 18, 150–60 CE, Czachesz (*Commission*, 120–22), earlier text revised in third century, Schäferdiek, 166–67, early third. Snyder, "Relationships" (forthcoming) offers a concise summary of different views.

81. See Junod-Kaestli (who argue for Egypt); Bremmer, "Women," 54–56 (Egypt); Czachesz, *Commission*, 120–22 (composed in Asia Minor, revised at Alexandria); Lalleman, *Acts of John*, 265–68; Schäferdiek, "Herkunft," Syria.

82. On this see under "Intertextuality," above.

certain type of Johannine tradition, but to locate it in Ephesus and establish John the son of Zebedee as the founder of that community. This item may be used in support of either Asia, where it would be linked to local issues, or of Syria, where anti-Paulinism had strong roots.[83] Because the earliest Acts—the canonical, APl, and APt—came from Asia, that region may have a slight advantage.

The decisive factor for dating the work is the circulation of the understanding that John the son of Zebedee wrote the fourth gospel and died a peaceful death in Ephesus, as the author seeks to capitalize upon this tradition rather than propound it.[84] The various elements of this legend emerge in the course of the second half of the second century but do not appear together before Irenaeus (approximately 180).[85] The primary edition of AJn is to be dated no earlier than approximately 190, with the expanded revision probably soon after 200. Many of its views (outside of those in chapters 94–102) could have been formulated in the time of the emperor Pius (138–61), but early theology does not mean an early date.[86] A work must be dated not earlier than its latest integral material.

THEOLOGY AND ETHOS[87]

The Narrative (apart from the embedded gospel and chapters 94–102; 109)

AJn proclaims one God, Jesus Christ, "the compassionate, the merciful, the holy, the pure, the undefiled, the immaterial, the only, the one, the unchanging" (chapter 107), and John as his prophet. With the exception of a portion of chapters 87–105 (treated below), which have a different literary and theological character, AJn cannot be described as representing one of the classi-

---

83. See Pervo, *Making of Paul*, 177–84; 187–98. A parallel is APt, set in Palestine and Rome, but originating in Asia Minor.

84. One feature of the tradition not exploited by AJn is that the apostle brought the mother of Jesus to Ephesus (cf. John 19:25–27). She would become the patron of the city: Vasiliki Limberis, "The Council."

85. See the clear analysis of Culpepper, *John*, 107–38. See also Trebilco, *Early Christians*, 237–92, and, most succinctly, Koester, "Ephesos," 135–39.

86. If this were the case, much of what televangelists have to offer could be dated before 50 CE.

87. Since the publication of Junod-Kaestli notable contributions have been made by the monographs of Sirker-Wicklaus, Schneider, and Lalleman, as well as in the various essays of Czachesz.

cal "gnostic" systems.[88] AJn does proclaim the one true God as invisible and immaterial, but it is not dualistic. Material reality is not fundamentally unreal or diabolic in origin.[89] Satanic reality is equally invisible and immaterial. The battleground between divine and diabolic is the human psyche. In classical theological terms AJn resemble "modalistic monarchianism,"[90] portray (particularly in chapters 94–102) a polymorphous Christ, and are somewhat docetic. These phenomena are early rather than late and are mutually compatible.

Docetism and Polymorphy. In the strict, upper-case D, sense, Docetism is the belief that Christ merely appeared to be human. In a broader sense all disinclinations to accept his full humanity can be labeled "docetic." Polymorphy assumes that a deity or other entities may assume any desired appearance. (Studies with abundant references to other works include Junod-Kaestli 2:491–93, Czachesz, *Commission*, 98–102, "Grotesque Body," and Lalleman, "Polymorphy.") These concepts were fashioned into tools by learned polytheists. A range of gods assimilated as one member of a pantheon could be portrayed as different manifestations of the same being. For polytheists the ability to change forms like hats was a property no god would do without. Docetism accompanied this capacity for metamorphosis: gods appearing in human form were not truly human. A feature shared with the Israelite tradition was the need to condescend to frail humans and the understanding that exposure to unalloyed deity was lethal. For polytheists these notions were not deviant, "heretical," or inappropriate.

Early Christians viewed the exalted Christ as endowed with the capacity to manifest divinity and the capacity for polymorphy. This lurks behind the recognition stories in John 20:11–18 and Luke 24:13–35, for example. When post-Easter stories that viewed the risen one as having cast off his human shackles went out of favor, they might be repurposed as incidents from Jesus' earthly career, as in Mark 6:45–52; 9:1–8.[91] Some strains of Christianity refused to abandon this understanding and extended it to cover the entire range of the

---

88. Those called "gnostics" would have only moderate difficulty in reading AJn as an expression of their tenets: Luttikhuizen, "Gnostic reading."

89. Ch. 79 invokes the "Lord of Creation." The contrast with a truly dualistic perspective is quite apparent in ch. 54.

90. The modalistic monarchians, or "Sabellians," maintained that apparent differentiation within the Godhead derived from successive modes of operations, e.g., God acted as father in creation, son in redemption, and spirit in sanctification. Examples occur in chs. 22, 24, 77, 82, 107, 108, 112.

91. See Robinson, "Jesus: From Easter to Valentinus."

Savior's career, including pre-existence, earthly sojourn, and glorification. Docetism was an effort to protect the divine from the corruption of mortal imperfection. Polymorphy could be deployed as an interpretive device: both as a means for showing divine transcendence, that God cannot be pinned down by human categories, and as a symbol of the multiple means God can use to communicate with pathetic mortals.

The theology of AJn shares these notions, but not necessarily from simply raiding the arsenal of pagan religion. The theology of AJn derives from primitive traditions pushed toward logical conclusions rather more than from the introduction of pagan or gnostic conceptualizations into the incarnational mainstream.

The "historical Jesus" of AJn 87–93, is, indeed, "God striding upon the earth,"[92] depicted without any need for qualification or apology, for gods should be gods and the manifestation of God in Christ would gain nothing from fleshly entanglement. The distance between the opponents of 1 John and AJn is not so far as to require the introduction of external systems of thought.[93] Those who classify this work as gnostic use the material in chapters 94–102 as the hermeneutical key to the whole.[94] Such interpretations suggest that the object of interpolating this material has been achieved, but they run counter to the normal methodological procedure utilized when one section of a document exhibits unique literary and theological characteristics. Portions thus identified are usually bracketed as probably secondary additions. This document requires at least a preliminary application of that method. When the peculiar material found in chapters 94–102 is set to one side, there are no convincing reasons for compressing the residue into a Valentinian or other "gnostic" mold.[95]

---

92. The phrase is from Käsemann's characterization of the interpretation of Ferdinand Christian Baur, in Käsemann, *The Testament of Jesus*, 9. Hengel has a similar conclusion (*Johannine Question*, 10).

93. For one reconstruction of the situation of 1 John and its aftermath see Raymond E. Brown, *The Epistles of John* (AB 30; Garden City, NY: Doubleday, 1982) 47–115. For discussion of Brown's reconstruction see Trebilco, *Early Christians*, 275–92. Note also Lalleman, *Acts of John*. A more recent study is von Wahlde, *Gospel and Letters*, 3:2–9, *et passim*. See also his *Johannine Commandments*.

94. Schäferdiek ("Acts of John," 2.165) offers a qualified criticism of this approach. See also Junod-Kaestli, 2:589–93, 680–82.

95. Valentinus flourished in the second quarter of the second century. He was a brilliant theologian and gifted writer, considered the founder of a school. His system was dualistic in conviction, focused upon the problem of the genesis of evil and escape from it. From him and his followers came the first commentaries on books later admitted into the NT.

Introduction

AJn also manifest aspects of a "benefactor Christology," found in Luke and, to a degree, in John,[96] another fairly primitive feature. This text proclaims a radical and rather concrete social and community ethic, of which sexual continence is only the bulwark. The catalogues of spiritual gifts in chapters 84 and 106 include life together and the sharing of property. Like the other ApocActs, AJn rejects any suggestions of compromise with the social order, an arrangement that would imprison souls under the cover of peace but through the reality of absolutizing the status quo. The pitiful condition of the "widows" of Ephesus (chapter 36) is a living charge against the Christian community, which John holds responsible for their welfare. Here, too, there are affinities with the Lukan perspective.[97]

Whereas the Fourth Gospel portrays a group in conflict with the synagogue over the Israelite heritage, and describes the other as "the Jews," AJn shows not a trace of interest in anything remotely tinged with salvation history. History does not seem to be a relevant category. The only society meriting consideration is the community of believers.

Said community gathers in the houses of its wealthy members, whose generosity does not generate the power of patronage for them (compare Luke 22:24–27, paralleled in Mark 10:42–44). This is a band of equals gathered around their apostolic missionary, whose powers they can share (by, for example, raising the dead). The positions occupied by women are both the symbol and the reality of community life. For officers there is no need.[98]

The faithful assemble for daily prayers (chapter 27), including a frequent eucharist with bread alone. The lack of regular reference to an initiation rite is noteworthy.[99] Initiation is by faith and brings full and immediate member-

---

96. See, e.g., AJn 108. The applicability of the benefactor model to Luke has been disseminated by Frederick W. Danker in a number of publications, e.g., *Jesus and the New Age*. For traces of a similar conception behind the Fourth Gospel see John 13:12–17.

97. A difference is that Luke is more concerned with summoning those with means to do their duty than is the author of AJn.

98. The departure scene, chs. 106–15, tries to remedy this. See the notes to the translation. Verus appears in ch. 30 as one "serving" John. This is a NT word for discipleship. When Verus is thereafter described as a "deacon," one suspects the presence of editorial modification to bring the structure into line with normative practice. This is no clue as to date, for the ApocActs in general portray "primitive" ecclesiastical structures. In the APl ecclesial terminology is less complex than in the epistles. Here, however, it conforms to the Fourth Gospel.

99. Chs. 94–102 supply the lacking initiatory rite, but not through a description of conventional baptism. The imposition of hands mentioned in ch. 46 includes all and is thus not part of a ritual initiation. 84:13 mentions the "holy bath" in conjunction with "eucharist." Ch. 57 has an interpolated reference to baptism.

ship in the community.[100] In effect, confession of Christ initiates. It would be unwise to imagine that AJn present actual and normative descriptions of Christian existence. If characters like Drusiana seem immune from temptation, backsliding is possible even for Andronikos and the possibility of temptation to apostatize is a leading subject of the exhortations. The percentage of magistrates' wives and other socially prominent converts in the first decades of Christian history was rather lower than the several Acts suggest. Was celibacy the norm for all or an ideal achieved by few? The former is not impossible, but celibacy may not have been an absolute requirement.[101] Pieter J. Lalleman holds that celibacy is not required for all in AJn, since the followers include married couples.[102] The neutral reader will not gain the impression that married life includes conjugal sex, but rather the opposite.

The Embedded Gospel
(Chapters 87–105 [109])

Formally this section does not resemble the usual patterns of the apocryphal acts, for it approaches in genre and content the revelatory gospels found at Nag Hammadi.[103] More specifically it is a reflex of the prototype of those gospels found in John 13–20, couched in the form of an apostolic reminiscence, like 2 Pet 1:16–18,[104] with a pastoral intent.

After the introductory scene in chapter 87, chapters 88–93 present reminiscences of John's experiences as a disciple. These include his call, the transfiguration, and other particular and general incidents, all presented as epiphanies.[105] The purpose of the recital is to demonstrate the full deity of Christ, past and present, and to recognize that, although this perplexed even

---

100. J. Snyder, *Language*, 107, shows that conversion is a process in AJn.
101. So, for example, the followers of Marcion, the early Christians of eastern Syria, Christian Manichaeans, many Gnostics of the classical types, Priscillianists, Bogomils, Albigensians, and Shakers, to name some of the Christian sects that have quite successfully demanded celibacy of their membership—all of which, to be sure, have died out.
102. Similarly, Klauck, "Acts of John," 43.
103. For a discussion of the genre see H. Koester, *Trajectories*, 193–98. An especially vivid example is the resemblance between AJn 97–100 and the *Second Treatise of the Great Seth*, NHC VII, 2:55, 30–56, 19, translated by Bullard and Gibbons in Robinson, *Nag Hammadi Library*, 365.
104. 2 Peter 1 in its entirety has much in common with the exhortations of AJn and helps give profile to the milieu of both.
105. Luke 5:1–11 already shows a tendency to present the call of the first disciples as an epiphany. AJn 93 shares the literary milieu of the multiplications of loaves (John 6:1–15 and parallels).

the disciples, it is a basis for confidence rather than for confusion. As Lalleman says, the *pathos* ("suffering" of Christ, for example, 96:32) involves all the activity of the Logos, including the cross.[106] This material also establishes John as the Beloved Disciple, that is, disciple *par excellence*, the favorite and intimate of Jesus, the recipient of choice revelation and thus, by implication, the bearer of the most authentic and unalloyed tradition.

In chapter 93 there begins an exhortation, concluded in 103-104. Chapters 94-102 interrupt this closing exhortation with a daring new edition of John 13-19. This fascinating interpolation presents a deeper and more sophisticated form of theological reflection than does the balance of AJn, with affinities to both Johannine thought and speculation related to (eastern) Valentinianism.[107]

AJn 87-105 reflect successive stages of conflict over the heritage of the Beloved Disciple. In effect the "witness" of John 19:34b and 21 here speaks from another side. AJn 87-105 is a counterblow to John 21. If chapters 87-93 and 103-105 stem from a relatively isolated perspective, the interpolator represents a Johannine wing that has received fresh stimulus and insight from "gnostic circles." The interpolation allows one to see the "edgy" Johannine tradition being pushed over the edge into the world of radical dualism and esoteric cosmology with its "great chain of being." Both early and additional components demonstrate, despite their divergence from the ultimately canonized texts, continuing debate over the meaning of the Fourth Gospel. As is now rather widely recognized, appreciation of "non-orthodox" Johannine Christianity requires study of AJn.[108]

The heretical character and extravagance notwithstanding, AJn possess a theological power and occasional sublimity that ought not to be denied. This is particularly true of 94-102, 109, whose author has a profound understanding of the metaphorical character and limitations of religious language and of the paradoxical nature of Christian belief, but it is not absent from the rest of the work, which is a sustained exercise in the understanding of Jesus'

---

106. Lalleman, *Acts of John*, 193.

107. On the origin and characteristics of chs. 94-102 (and 109) see Junod-Kaestli, 2:581-677; Schneider, *Mystery*; and Lalleman, *Acts of John*, to name some of the major studies. Note also Roldanus, "Eucharistie," who has many solid theological observations. Classification of this material as a subsequent addition does not mean that it must be later than or that it cannot contain traditions at least as early as the more integral parts of the book.

108. Witness Lalleman and Trebilco. Even four decades ago conservative scholars were likely to reject the claim that apocryphal texts could be of value for constructing the history of the Johannine community.

deeds and words as parabolic, and of the extension of those "parables" into the present.[109]

AJn, like ATh and AAn, presents a distinct and intriguing theology. These three ApocActs are important testimonies to the diversity of early Christianity. They have survived to the extent that they have, because of the appeal of their narratives and the value of these stories for religious edification. Where tracts and treatises perished quickly in flames or slowly by moths, these books endured because they were interesting.

Reception of the Acts of John

Apart from versions and the preparation of manuscripts (an indication of considerable interest), little is heard after Photius in the east.[110] Knowledge of the Manichaean collection appears to have faded in the Latin west, but the Celtic Christians of Ireland enjoyed apocrypha;[111] their missionaries evidently transmitted this interest to Anglo-Saxon England.[112] Benedictine interest in educational renewal later motivated edifying sermons that utilized Johannine apocrypha. R. Bremmer has translated Ælfric's (approximately 1000) sermon on St. John's Day (27 December).[113] The miracle at Cana (John 2:1–12) so inspired the groom that he abandoned his bride and followed Jesus in his virginal state. The groom's name was John.

A tenth-century nun, Hrotsvitha of Gandersheim, wrote a half-dozen Latin plays to compete with Terence.[114] One, *Calimachus,* was based upon the tale of Drusiana and Kallimachos (AJn 63–86).[115] This drama comprised nine scenes. Hrotsvitha semi-defended the use of apocryphal texts, an indication that her practice had received some criticism.[116]

The dinner dance that replaces the Last Supper (AJn 94–96), first published in 1897, received attention in the twentieth century. Gustav Holst set it to music, using some plainsong hymns for Holy Week, in his 1917 *Hymn*

---

109. For my understanding see Pervo, "Johannine Trajectories."
110. See also Appendix C to the translation. The major study of reception is Junod and Kaestli's *L'histoire.*
111. See the works of MacNamara.
112. Rolf Bremmer, "Reception," is a fascinating account.
113. Rolf Bremmer, "Reception," 188–96. The Latin title, *Assumptio,* is equivalent to Greek *Metastasis.*
114. Hrotsvitha has inspired a Brill companion, edited by P. Brown. See also Rose, *Ritual Memory.* The dramatist's work is also noted by Konstan, "Acts of Love."
115. The Latin *Virtutes* (= miracles) *Iohannis* contains a close translation of this story. See Appendix C.
116. For other examples see Junod and Kaestli, *L'histoire,* 104–7.

Introduction 23

of Jesus, dedicated to Ralph Vaughn Williams. Holst made his own translation for this still popular work.[117] Luis Buñuel's film *La Voie Lacté* (*The Milky Way*) depicted some followers of Priscillian performing the dance (prior to an orgy).[118] Marguerite Yourcenar utilizes this text in her mystical novel, *The Abyss*.[119]

---

117. I am unaware of an earlier English version.
118. The orgy repeats ecclesiastical slander. Although Priscillianists read AJn, there is no evidence that they performed the dance.
119. Trans. from French by G. Frick (New York: Farrar, Strauss & Giraud, 1977).

HOW TO USE THIS BOOK

46   *Acts of John 98:7–100:6*

98:9 ¹1 Cor 15:24; Eph 1:21; 6:12; Col 2:10, 15; AJn 98:9
² Cf. 36:4
99:2 ²Cf. 97:6
³ ► 98:3
99:3 ²Cf. Mk 8:27–28; Mt 13–14; Lk 9:18–19   ⟵ Cross references

terms and put into words for your benefit, is the proper distinction of all, the secure recovery of what is well-rooted from amidst what is uncertain; ‹in short,› the disposition of Wisdom. ⁸"When Wisdom's disposition is present, those on the right ‹side› come to be—but also those on the left:ᵃ ⁹authorities, principalities,ᵃ demons, forces, threats,ᵇ passions, accusations, Satan, and the lower root; from this last arises the nature of created entities.

99 ¹"This cross, then, which has anchored all by word and separated out what derives from creation and the inferior, and has then permeated all things, is not the wooden cross you will behold when you go down from this place. ²Nor am I the one upon the cross,ᵃ I whom you do not see, but whose voice alone you hear.ᵇ ³I was imagined to be what I am not, since I am not who the masses think I am.ᶜ ⁴What they shall say about me is beneath me and unfitting to my station. ⁵Since, then, the place of rest is beyond your powers of sight or speech, I, its Lord, am even more indescribable and ineffable.

100 ¹"The crowd without distinct form around the cross is the lower nature. ²If not all those whom you saw on the cross have a single form, that is because not every member of the one who has come down has yet been gathered. ³When, however, the essential reality of authentic humanity, the race which cleaves to me in obedience to my voice, is taken up to glory, those who hear me now will be together with that race, no longer as they are now, but above the cross—just as I am now above it. ⁴For so long as you do not identify yourself as belonging to me, I am not that which I was. ⁵But if you listen to me, you will be like me, and I shall be what I was [...]. ⁶So take no thought for the masses, and treat with contempt those who

⟵ Acts of John translation

100:3 • Similarly, Clement of Alexandria, *Excerpts from Theodotus* 26.3.
100:6 • *all that I am ...*: This concluding phrase (με ὅλον παρὰ τῷ πατρὶ καὶ τὸν πατέρα παρ' ἐμοί) is strongly reminiscent of Jn 10:30; 14:11 (cf. 17:21), and is introduced with a verb of knowing (γίνωσκε) that likewise recalls Jn 10:38 (ἵνα γνῶτε καὶ γινώσκητε [v.1. πιστεύσητε]). AJn 100:6 adds the word ὅλον, which here may be taken either adjectivally (as in the present translation: "all of me") or adverbially ("I am in the Father *completely*"). This longer version of the saying occurs, probably independently, in Ep apost 17.4, and is quoted by later authors (e.g., Augustine *Serm.* 9).   ⟵ Notes on translation

98:8 Lallemann proposes to emend the text with a negative: "not present," *Acts of John*, 192. He does not justify this change on the grounds of textual criticism, but holds that it produces better sense.
100:5 *what I was ...*: The text is corrupt, in that there is a small lacuna.

⟵ Notes on original language manuscripts

25

THE ACTS OF JOHN

EPISODE 1

LACUNA I

The beginning of the Acts is lost. The text presumably opened in Palestine, either with a meeting at which the apostles cast lots for their mission areas, as in several other apocryphal acts, or with an appearance to John and James by the risen Lord on the Lake of Galilee, as in John 21. AJn 113 refers to such an incident, possibly suppressed in the opening because of its attitude toward marriage in general and its representation of John's superiority to the other disciples. Perhaps the events to which *Pseudo-Titus* quotation 3 refers belongs here (see below, Appendix 1). Somewhat less likely is that the narrative began by describing how John was exiled to Patmos, followed by his release and journey to Miletus. See the Introduction. The extant text opens in Part 2, when John is in Miletus.

EPISODE 2

FROM EPHESUS TO MILETUS

18:1 ᵃCf. 55:2
18:5 ᵃCf. Lk 2:29; ATh 3:1
ᵇCf. Mt 6:10; 26:42; Lk 11:2; ATh 3:1
19:2 ᵃCf. Lk 1:63
19:3 ᵃCf. Jn 9:3

18 Impelled by a vision, John was in haste to get to Ephesus, and so it was only with some difficulty that Damonikos, a relative of his named Aristodemos, one Kleobios (who was very wealthy) and the wife of Marcellus could prevail on him to spend a day at rest with them in Miletus.ᵃ ²They had set out then at the crack of dawn and had already made four miles when a voice, audible to all of us, boomed from heaven: ³"John, you are going to give your Lord glory in Ephesus, glory you will discover, you and all the believers with you, as well as some who will come to faith through you."

⁴Because he realized just what he was to encounter at Ephesus, John, filled with inner joy, replied, ⁵"See, Lord, I move onward in obedience to your will.ᵃ Let what you want come to pass."ᵇ

19 As we drew near to the city, a principal Ephesian magistrate, a nobleman named Lykomedes, came to meet us. ²He fell at the feet of John, saying, "Your name is John.ᵃ ³The god you proclaim has sent you on a mission of kindness to my wife, who has been paralyzed for seven days now and lies without chance of cure: glorify your god by healing herᵃ out of compassion for us. ⁴I had come to the point of considering suicide, but then someone appeared beside me with these words: 'Lykomedes, turn back from this terrible idea that haunts you! Don't let it have mastery over you. ⁵Out of compassion for my servant Kleopatra I have dispatched from Miletus a man named John: he will raise her and give her back to you, safe and sound.' ⁶So then, don't delay, servant of the god who revealed your very self to me, but come quickly to my wife, who has scarcely a breath left in her."

18:1 • *Impelled by a vision:* Modern editors are in agreement that the material printed in Bonnet as AJn 1–17 does not belong to the ancient text.
18:3 • *believers* (ἀδελφοί): "brothers (and sisters)," but in Christian literature of this period a technical term for believers.
18:3 • *some:* For the modest understatement regarding "some" rather than "all" believing, see also 22:8; 30:7; ATh 9:5; 141:6; and already Rom 11:14.
19:2 • *Your name is John,* usually translated as a question (following Bonnet's punctuation), is here taken as a statement of divinely-granted insight: the nobleman knows whom to expect and says, in effect, "You must be John!"

Acts of John 19:7–21:4

⁷John immediately set out from the city gate for Lykomedes house, together with him and the company of believers[a] with whom he had traveled. ⁸Kleobios, for his part, told his servants, "Go ahead to my relative Kallippos and see to it that he makes suitable arrangements to entertain us, so that I and his son, whom I accompanied here, shall find all in good order."

20 When Lykomedes had come with John to <his> house, where his wife lay sick, he grasped John's feet once more and cried out, "Sir, cast your eyes on this faded beauty. ²See how young she is! See this poor wife of mine, the fabled flower that once drove all Ephesus wild! ³Poor me, smashed by envy, crushed, smitten by the eyes of my enemies! ⁴Sure, it's well within my capacity to harm many people, but I've never done anyone an injustice,[a] and I've taken care not to observe any evil or misfortune like the present, anticipating just this sort of event. ⁵So what benefit has my careful planning earned me, Kleopatra? What profit has the pious repute in which I've been held to this very day brought me? ⁶Seeing you lying in such a wretched state, I suffer more than the godless, Kleopatra. ⁷Alright: the sun will never glimpse me again in its daily course, not if you're no longer my intimate—I'll go ahead of you, Kleopatra, and free myself from life. ⁸Youth and good health I reckon as nothing; I'll plead my case at the bar of Justice as one who has served with justice—although I could bring Her to justice for judging with injustice! ⁹As a pale shade of a living being I'll wreak my revenge on Her: I'll say to Her, 'You've robbed me of light by wresting Kleopatra from me.¹⁰You've made of me a corpse by providing me with this "gift." ¹¹You've driven me to spit in the face of Providence by cutting off my source of confidence.'"

21 As he continued to address Kleopatra, Lykomedes came near to her couch and broke into loud cries of woe. ²But John then pulled him back: "Give up these laments and unsuitable words of yours," he said. "It's not fitting that you should distrust what has been revealed to you. ³Be assured: you'll get your wife back. Stand with us, who have come <here> because of her, and pray to the God you saw me reveal in a dream. ⁴So then, Lykomedes, rouse yourself—yes, you! Open your soul; throw off this deep sleep; beg the Lord, plead with him on behalf of your spouse, and he will raise her."

19:7 [a]Cf. 18:3
20:4 [a]Cf. ATh 62:4

20:8 • *Her*, i.e., "Justice" (Δικη), the personification of what is orderly and right, as in Hesiod *Theog.* 902; Aeschylus *Sept. c. Theb.* 662.

21:6 ᵃCf. ATh 44:4
22:3 ᵃCf. 108:2; ATh 95:8; 156:3
22:7 ᵃCf. Acts 3:6
ᵇCf. 45:3
22:8 ᵃ ⇁ 18:3

⁵But <Lykomedes> fell to the floor and wept without restraint <and so expired>.

⁶In tears John exclaimed, "Never was a vision so traduced, never such a test contrived against me, never such a web of intrigue devised to entrap me.ᵃ ⁷Was it for this that the voice that came to me on the road set about its work? Did one intent on betraying me to this mass of citizenry because of Lykomedes disclose to me what would happen here? ⁸The fellow lies lifeless and, as for me, I know full well that I shan't be allowed to leave this house alive. ⁹Why the delay, Lord? Why have you kept back from us your gracious promise? ¹⁰I beg you, Lord, don't give any reason for the one who revels in the misfortunes of others to exult; don't give the one who mocks us any chance to dance for joy. ¹¹No! Let your holy name and mercy hurry to our side: raise up these two lifeless bodies brought into being to discredit me."

22

While John was shouting this out, all Ephesus dashed to the house of Lykomedes, presuming that he had died. ²So when John saw the huge mob that had gathered, he said to the Lord, "Now is the time for comfort and confidence in you, Christ! ³Now is the time for us who are harassed to receive help from you, the healer who freely bestows your curative power.ᵃ ⁴Keep my coming to this house from ridicule: I beg you, Jesus, help this great multitude to come to you, the ruler of all things. ⁵See this tribulation; see those who are prostrate here. And make from those here assembled sacred vessels for your ministry, because they will have seen what you so freely bestow. ⁶For you, Christ, you yourself said, 'Ask—it'll be given to you.' ⁷So we ask you, King, not for gold, silver,ᵃ property, or possession, nor for any perishable earthly object, but for two souls through whom you will turn those coming to faithᵇ toward your way, toward your instruction, toward your assurance, toward your most noble promise. ⁸Someᵃ of them will be saved, when they have come to discover your majesty through your revival of the lifeless;

21:5 • *fell to the floor* (πεσὼν ἐπὶ τοῦ ἐδαφοῦς): also in 24:8.
21:5 • *<and so expired>* is inferred from 21:8; 22:1.
22:2 • *time for comfort*, or "time of refreshment" (καιρὸς ἀναψύξεως): The phrase recalls the sole NT occurrence of the noun ἀνάψυξις, in Acts 3:20, there in the plural: "*times* of refreshment" (the cognate verb is likewise found only once, in 2 Tim 1:16). It is found with the definite article (τῆς) in Origen *Schol. in Cant.* 4.5, of "spiritual refreshment in this age" (LPGL, s.v. καιρός 2 [p. 693b]); in the LXX only at Exod 8:15(11) "when the Pharaoh saw that there was a *respite*"; also Isa 28:12 Aq. (LXX ἀνάπαυμα) and 32:15 Sm.
22:6 • *Ask—it'll be given to you*: αἰτεῖτε καὶ δοθήσεται ὑμῖν, as in Mt 7:7; Lk 11:9; cf. Jn 16:24. The exhortation recurs, in its tripartite synoptic form, in ATh 53:8.

you, then, provide hope directed toward you. ⁹So, then, I'm going to approach Kleopatra and say, 'Arise in the name of Jesus Christ.'"ª

23 He went up, touched her face, and said, "Kleopatra, the one who speaks to you is the one whom every <supernatural> ruler fears, and every creature, every power, all depth and darkness alike, grim-visaged death, the vaults of heaven and the caverns of hell: ²resurrection of the dead and giving of sight to the blind, all the power of the prince of this world, and the arrogance of its ruler. ³Get up! Cease being an excuse to the multitudes unwilling to believe and a trial to souls capable of hope and salvation."

⁴Right away Kleopatra cried out loudly, "I'm getting up, master. Save your Kleopatra!" ⁵And Ephesus was convulsed at the marvelous spectacle of a woman arisen after seven days <on her death bed>.

⁶Kleopatra inquired after her husband. John replied, "Kleopatra, if you keep your soul unshaken and unperturbed, you will soon have your spouse Lykomedes standing here beside you [...], ⁷if indeed you are not agitated or disturbed by what has happened and keep faith in my God, who will through my agency give him back alive. ⁸Come then with me to your other bedroom and you will see him who had died rise again by the power of my God."

24 After Kleopatra had entered her bedroom with John and seen Lykomedes dead for her sake, she could make no sound, but ground her teeth, bit her tongue, and closed her eyes, pouring forth a rain of tears, yet still quietly heeding the apostle. ²John's heart went out to Kleopatra when he saw how she did not rant or rave, and he called upon that perfect compassion which demands nothing for itself: ³"Lord Jesus, you see this self-control; you see this restraint; you see Kleopatra crying out in the silent depths of her soul. She encloses within herself feelings that are unbearable. ⁴My soul prophesies, O Master: I know that this woman is near death because of Lykomedes."

⁵She calmly answered, "That I intend, master. Nothing else."

⁶Drawing near to the couch upon which Lykomedes lay, John took Kleopatra's hand and said, "Kleopatra, because of the huge

22:9 ªCf. Acts 2:38; 3:6; 4:10; 10:48; 16:18; 1 Cor 5:4; Col 3:17; 2 Thess 3:6

24:2 • *perfect compassion ... itself*, or, more literally, "perfect and prideless mercy" (τὰ τέλεια σπλάγχνα καὶ ἀνυπερήφανα): for similar epithets see 52:1; 108:3; AcTh 48:1.

24:6 *Drawing near ...*: About sixteen letters are illegible in H.

24:6 ᵃCf. Jn 11:42	
24:7 ᵃCf. Mt 8:22; Lk 9:60	
26:3 ᵃCf. Lk 14:21; 1 Cor 4:19; Phil 2:24; 2 Tim 4:19	
ᵇCf. Heb 11:8	

crowd standing hereᵃ and because of your relatives also present, say to your husband in a loud voice: ⁷'Get up and glorify God's name, which restores the "dead" to the "dead."'"ᵃ

⁸She approached, spoke as directed, and raised him up at once; and as for him, having got up he fell to the floor and attempted to kiss John's feet. ⁹The latter, however, lifted him up, saying, "Kiss not my feet, you misguided fellow. Kiss rather the feet of the God by whose power you have both been raised."

25 Lykomedes replied, "I entreat and adjure you in the name of the God through whom you raised us that you lodge with us—you and your companions [...]."

²Kleopatra, for her part, grasped his feet and made the same entreaty.

³"I'll be with you tomorrow," John said.

⁴They nonetheless persisted: "Your God has no hope to offer us. If you do not stay with us, we shall have been raised in vain."

⁵Now Kleobios, joined by Aristodemos and Damonikos as well, became quite agitated and urged John, "Let's stay with them, so that they'll stay with the Lord and not be led astray." ⁶So John and the believers stayed there.

26 A large crowd had gathered, drawn by John. While he was addressing those present, Lykomedes dashed off to a friend who was a clever artist and said, ²"See how much I have troubled myself by coming in person! ³Come quicklyᵃ now to my house and do a portrait of the person I indicate. He must not knowᵇ of it."

⁴As he handed the requisite implements and pigments to an attendant, the artist replied, "Point him out to me and don't worry about anything else." ⁵Lykomedes showed the artist who John was

---

24:8 • *attempted to kiss* (κατεφίλει), understood as a conative imperfect.
24:9 • *feet of the God:* This striking anthropomorphism is anticipated, e.g., in Eph 1:22; Heb 2:8; Rev 19:10. Cf. also Acts 10:26.
25:3 • *tomorrow,* or possibly "until tomorrow"; but 25:4 suggests that what is at stake is the invitation to stay for the present night.
26–29 • The story about the portrait (AJn 26–29) represents a common philosophical theme connected to the contrast between appearance and reality. A close parallel is Porphry's (c. 234–c. 305) *Life of Plotinus* 1. See Junod-Kaestli 2.448-52. A related debate was the issue of images to represent the gods, ably defended by Dio Chrysostom *Or.* 12. Christian opposition to images could claim the support of some philosophical circles. See Origen *C. Celsum* 3.15. This attitude led to the condemnation of AJn in 787. See the Introduction.

25:1 *your companions ...*: H contains ca. sixteen illegible letters at this point.

and located him in a spot nearby from which the apostle of Christ was visible. ⁶He kept himself close to the blessed one, banqueting on the faith and knowledge of our God, happier yet that he would possess John in a portrait.

27 That day the artist sketched an outline and left. ²After adding the colors on the next day he delivered the finished portrait to a delighted Lykomedes, who placed it in his bedroom, wreathed with flowers. ³In due course John began to notice something and said, "My beloved child, what do you do alone in your room after coming from the bath? ⁴Shouldn't you be present with the other believers when I offer prayer? Are you avoiding us?" ⁵Speaking thus and teasing Lykomedes, he entered the chamber. ⁶There he saw a garlanded portrait of an elderly man with lamps beside it and altars in front of it. ⁷Addressing Lykomedes he said, "What do you intend with this portrait? Is some god of yours depicted here? ⁸I see that you are, in fact, still following pagan ways!"

⁹Lykomedes replied, "The only God I acknowledge is the one who raised me from death with my wife. ¹⁰If, however, it is right and proper that, next to God, our earthly benefactors be acknowledged as gods—¹¹you are the one depicted in this painting, you whom I crown and kiss and revere, you who are my guide on the path to good."

28 Then John (who had never before glimpsed his own face) said, "You are teasing me, dear boy. Do I look like this? ²How in your Lord's name are you going to convince me that this portrait looks like me?"

³Lykomedes then brought him a mirror. ⁴After seeing himself in it and scrutinizing the portrait he exclaimed, "As Jesus Christ lives, the portrait is like me! ⁵In another sense it is not, my child, but merely like my physical appearance. ⁶For if this painter who has copied my face wishes to capture me in a portrait, he would at present be unable to find the necessary pigments, or boards on which to paint, and model, dress, shape, the right configuration—whether as old man or youth—in short, everything that is visible to the senses.

29 "Now you be a good painter for me, Lykomedes. ²You have pigments given you through me by Jesus, who would make of us

---

27:8 • *following pagan ways* (ἐθνικῶς ζῶντα): cf. Gal 2:14; this rare adverb appears also in Clement of Alexandria *Stromateis* 6.5; 7.14.

all portraits for himself: he knows the shapes, forms, figures, dispositions, and patterns of our souls. ³I shall tell you what to paint with these hues: faith in God, knowledge, godly fear, love, sharing, meekness, goodness, mutual concern, purity, sincerity, tranquility, lack of anxiety, absence of grief, dignity—⁴the whole palette of pigments that portray your soul, paints that even now are lifting up your dejected limbs and pressing down those which have been too haughty [... ⁵which] nurse your injuries and heal your wounds, dress your unkempt hair, scrub your face, teach your eyes what to look for, cleanse your insides, purge your stomach, and excise your nether organs. ⁶Quite simply: when a full blend and mixture of colors like these has made its mark upon your soul, it will present it indelible, firm, and without rough edges unto our Lord Jesus Christ. ⁷But what you have accomplished here is childish and inadequate: you have painted a lifeless image of a lifeless person [...]. ⁸[Make rather] an image of a living being in a living soul. ⁹Now, things like this are unworthy of serious attention; all such things are ridiculous. ¹⁰Let us for our part be concerned with matters that are worthy of serious attention ...]."

30 John then directed one Verus, his servant and a believer, to gather the elderly women from throughout Ephesus. ²Verus, together with Kleopatra and Lykomedes, made preparations for their care, and then returned with this report: ³"John, I have found but four women over sixty in good physical condition in this place; the rest are paralyzed, deaf, arthritic, or afflicted with one illness or another."

⁴After John had heard this information he was silent for a while; then, rubbing his face[a] in distress, he exclaimed, "What slackness Ephesus has exhibited! ⁵What flabbiness in conduct and inadequacy in response to God! What an object of derision you have been making all this time of the faithful in Ephesus, Satan! ⁶Jesus, who gives me his favor and freely grants me his boldness, is silently telling me now, 'Summon the old women who are ill, go with them to the theater, and heal them through me. ⁷I shall make of these healings a good end by using them to convert some[a] of the people who will come to see a display.'"

29:4 *too haughty ...*: About sixty-five letters in H are illegible.
29:7 *a lifeless person:* The balance of this address is lost. Only a few words are decipherable, permitting the partial and tentative reconstruction of the next two verses following Junod-Kaestli, 1. 180.

31 John bade farewell to the entire crowd gathered on his account at Lykomedes' with these words: ²"All who wish to view the power of God, assemble in the theater tomorrow."

³By dawn the crowd had already formed. When the Roman governor learned what was happening, he, too, hastened to take his place among the multitude.

⁴Now a certain chief magistrate and leading Ephesian citizen of that period named Andronikos was circulating a rumor that John had promised impossible and incredible things. ⁵"Well," he proposed, "if he has in mind anything of the sort I am hearing about, let him come naked into the theater, that being a public and open place, carrying nothing in his hands. ⁶Further, let him not utter the magical name I have heard him employ."

32 Despite learning of this and being irritated by these words, John directed that the elderly women be carried to the theater. ²When all had been brought in, some on their cots, others lying nearly comatose there, before a populace mobilized by excitement, everyone fell silent. ³When it was very still, John opened his mouth and began to speak:

33 "Good people of Ephesus, let me explain at the outset why I have come to visit your city [...] or what has made me so audacious as to display myself to you all in this public assembly. ²In fact, my embassy has no merely human purpose, nor is my visit frivolous. ³I do not come like a merchant engaged in sale or exchange.ᵃ ⁴Rather, I am here to convert all of you who have been imprisoned by unbelief and enslaved to shameful desires. ⁵Jesus Christ, whose herald I am, will convert you. He is compassionate and good and intends to deliver you from error. ⁶By his power I shall reprove unbelief,

33:3 ªCf. 2 Cor 2:17

31:2 • *the power of God* (τὴν τοῦ θεοῦ δύναμιν) is the title boasted by Simon Magus in Acts 8:10 ἡ δύναμις τοῦ θεοῦ. The phrase recurs at the conclusion to this section (see below, Lacuna ii).
31:3 • *Roman governor*: P. Oxy. 850 (see Appendix A, below) refers to a Roman governor, but it is difficult to correlate this reference to the events in progress.
33:1 • *Good people of Ephesus* (Ἄνδρες Ἐφέσιοι): The Greek phrase recurs in 36:5; 39:1, 5; 43:2; in the NT only at Acts 19:35 (but there are comparable expressions in Acts 2:14; 3:12; 17:22). The pleonastic "men" typically indicates the speaker's respect for the audience, hence the present translation.

32:2 *others ... there*: The text of this phrase is corrupt.

33:1 *your city*: After *your city* about thirty lines are illegible in H.

even that of your chief magistrate, by raising up these women of your city now lying before you. ⁷You all see how wretched is their condition and how serious their maladies. It is not possible for me at present. [⁸Even though they are on the verge of death, they will actually participate in the healing.]

34

"Before that I should like to plant something in your ears: concern for the state of your souls. This is why I have come to you. ²[I do not wish you to imagine] that this present time, which is actually a period of subjugation, will last forever, nor to lay up treasures on earth, where all fades away[a] [...]; ³nor to suppose that if you have children you will find security in them, nor for their sake to engage in sharp practice[a] and always seek more acquisitions [...]; ⁴nor should you who are poor lament if you can't find means to support your pleasures, for even those who do have such means consider you lucky if they fall ill. ⁵Don't rejoice, you wealthy, because you have numerous possessions: through your acquisition of them you store up endless grief for yourselves in the event that you lose them. ⁶Not only that, but so long as they are yours, you live gripped with the fear that someone will attack you because of them.

35

"Think of this, you who delight in physical beauty and look down on others: the sure and promised goal of the grave. ²Take note of this, you who live it up in adultery: natural and statute law alike will exact their due, and conscience even earlier <than that>. ³And you, adulterous woman: in setting yourself against the law you don't know what your outcome will be. ⁴You, too, who have money on deposit but don't share it with the needy: you will find no one to offer mercy when, having shuffled off this mortal coil, you burn in torment, badly in need of mercy.[a] ⁵Take note of this, you who rage with anger, that you are acting like brute beasts. ⁶Realize, you contentious drunkard, that you are losing your senses in subjection to a shameful and filthy desire.

36

"You who take indulgent pleasure in gold, in ivory, and jewels: can you see the object of your passion when darkness falls?

34:2 ᵃCf. Mt 6:19
34:3 ᵃ ⇥ 68:2; ATh 12:3
35:4 ᵃCf. Lk 16:19–35

33:8 *Even though ...*: The lacuna represents ca. forty-five illegible letters in H; hence the words in square brackets are only one possible reconstruction of the sense.
34:2 *I do not wish ...*: About forty letters of H are illegible at the beginning of the verse, and about thirty-five at the end; the bracketed phrase is again conjectural.
34:3 *seek more acquisitions:* About forty letters are illegible in H here.

²You who are in thrall to fine clothes—suppose that you die: will they be of any use where you are headed? ³Know this, murderer, that after death you will receive the punishment you deserve, and in double measure. ⁴So, too, you poisoner, dabbler in magic, swindler, thief, pervert, crook, and all of this ilk: your deeds will lead you into unquenchable fire[a] and vast darkness, into a chasm of torment and endless menace.[b] ⁵So then, good people of Ephesus,[a] change your ways, for you know full well that emperors, princes, and tyrants, those who boast of their accomplishments and they who wage wars—they'll depart this world naked and wail together in eternal afflictions."

36:4 [a] Cf. Mk 9:43
[b] Cf. 98:9
36:5 [a] → 33:1

EPISODE 3

LACUNA II

There is a gap at this point, which must have included the first story about Drusiana and Andronikos. Since, according to AJn 31, Andronikos is a chief magistrate and antagonistic toward John, it is not improbable that his wife, Drusiana, is converted by seeing the wondrous healings (82:6). After conversion she declines marital relations. Andronikos first seeks to entice her with his fortune (63:4) and then condemns her to death, locking her in a tomb with John. This adventure, by no means unique to the *Acts of John* (see, for example, AcTh 115; AcAnPas 22–23), may have been suppressed because of the polymorphous christology it contained (see 87:2). Perhaps the contents of P. Oxy. 850 belong here also. See the Introduction.

An ancient copyist who found the passage incomplete, or who personally abbreviated the text, added the following to complete AJn 36:

⁶After he had said these things, John healed all their illnesses by the power of God.

36:5 • *naked:* In this respect, therefore, these powerful people share the common lot of humankind (see Job 1:21; Eccl 5:15; cf. 1 Tim 6:7).

EPISODE 4

A DEUTERO-JOHANNINE "BOOK OF GLORY"

87:2 ᵃCf. APl 9.20; APt 5:27; ATh 27:11
87:3 ᵃCf. 45:2
88:2 ᵃCf. Jn 21:25
88:3 ᵃCf. APt 20:12; ATh 53
88:4 ᵃCf. Jn 1:40–42
ᵇCf. Mt 4:18-22; Mk 1:16–20
88:6 ᵃ ⇀ 89:1

87 Now those present attempted to learn the reason for what had happened. ²In particular they were perplexed at Drusiana's statement, "The Lord appeared to me when I was in the tomb. He resembled John and resembled a youth."ᵃ ³Since they were in such confusion, and in some respects insufficiently formed in their faithᵃ to grasp this firmly, John explained:

88 "My fellow believers, you have experienced nothing unusual or remarkable in this mode of perceiving the Lord, since even we, whom he chose as his apostles, were subject to numerous tests. ²There are things I have personally seen and heard that are beyond my capacity to relate or to put in writing to you.ᵃ ³I must now adjust myself to your ears and share with you according to your individual capacitiesᵃ things you are able to hear, so that you may perceive the glory that engulfs him, glory which was, is now, and will be forever. This is what I mean:

⁴"After he had chosen Peter and Andrew, two brothers,ᵃ he approached my brother James and me and said, 'I have need of you. Come to me.'ᵇ ⁵My brother heard this and asked, 'John, what does this child who is calling to us from the shore want?'

⁶"'What child?'ᵃ

⁷"'The one gesturing to us.'

87:1 • For the location of AJn 87–105 and its relation to the ancient *Acts of John*, see the Introduction above. A copyist supplied this superscript to these chapters: The marvelous account of his deeds and the visions received by Saint John the Divine from our Lord Jesus Christ. The account relates how he first appeared to Peter and James, and in it is narrated the mystery of the cross.

87:2 • *to me* is emphatic: μοι ὁ κύριος ὤφθη; contrast, e.g., Lk 24:34 ὤφθη Σίμωνι; 1 Cor 15:5.

87:2 • *resembled* translates Greek ὡς.

88:1 • *My fellow believers:* The Greek phrase (Ἄνδρες ἀδελφοί), in the NT confined to the book of Acts (1:16; 2:29, 37; 7:2, 26; 13:15, 26, 38; 15:7, 13; 22:1; 23:1, 6; 28:17), occurs also in 4 Macc 8:19.

88:3 • *This is what I mean* translates γάρ, the second word of the next sentence; what follows explains John's enigmatic remark about what he has seen and heard.

⁸"'We've spent too much time out on the water. You can't see straight, James. Don't you see a man, well-built, handsome, and cheerful-looking?'

⁹"'I don't. But let's go and see what this is about.'

¹⁰"As we brought the boat to shore, we observed that he helped us get it securely beached.

89 "After we had left that spot, determined to follow him, he appeared to me still differently: almost bald, with a thick, flowing beard, but to James as a youth[a] whose beard had just begun to come in. ²We were both confused about the meaning of this apparition; and as we kept following, we became more and more confused in our struggle to comprehend what had happened.

³"But then I saw something even more astonishing. My efforts to view him more closely led me to see that his eyes never blinked; they were constantly open. ⁴Often he seemed to me to be both a small, unattractive person and one always looking at everything in the sky. ⁵He had another remarkable quality: at table he would let me lie on his chest;[a] I would nestle closely. ⁶Sometimes his chest would feel smooth and soft; at other times, hard as a rock. ⁷This left me confused, wondering, 'What does this mean?' ⁸As I wrestled in my mind about this he [...].

90 "On another occasion he had James, Peter, and me accompany him to the mountain on which he used to pray.[a] ²There we saw upon him a kind of light that a mortal using perishable speech could not possibly describe. ³Similarly, at another time, he led the three of us up the mountain, saying, 'Come with me.' ⁴Again we went, and stood at some distance watching him pray.[a] ⁵And then, because he loved me,[a] I quietly approached him, supposing that I was not detected, and stood gazing at him from behind. ⁶He was quite without clothing, devoid of the garments we usually saw him wearing; in fact, he wasn't like a regular person in any way. ⁷His feet were whiter than snow—so bright that they illumined the ground

89:1 [a]Cf. 88:6; APt 21:13
89:5 [a]Cf. Jn 13:23, 25
90:1 [a]Cf. Mk 9:2–8; Mt 17:1–8; Lk 9:28–36; ATh 143:8
90:4 [a]Cf. Lk 9:28–29
90:5 [a]Cf. Jn 20:2

89:8 • *As I wrestled in my mind ...:* The reply of Christ has been lost. If this is due to theological censorship, the contents may have been remarkable.

90:5 • *from behind* (εἰς τὰ ὀπίσθια) recalls Exod 33:23, where Moses is told by God, "you shall see my back (LXX τὰ ὀπίσω); but my face shall not be seen."

90:6 • Gods and heroes were regularly portrayed as naked.

90:6 • *a regular person,* literally, "he was completely unlike a human being" (ἄνθρωπον δὲ οὐδὲ ὅλως).

90:7 • *whiter than snow* (χιόνος λευκοτέρους): This biblical idiom (see, e.g., Ps 51:7 [50:9] ὑπὲρ χιόνα λευκανθήσονται; Isa 1:18 ὡς χιόνα λευκανῶ; Dan 7:9 Th ὡσεὶ χιὼν λευκόν; Mt 28:3; Rev 1:14) complements the reference to the feet of God in 24:9.

90:8 ᵃCf. Jn 20:27
90:12 ᵃCf. Jas 1:13
93:3 ᵃCf. Lk 7:36; 11:37; 14:1

beneath him. ⁸His head extended up to the sky. I cried out in terror. He turned around, like a small person in appearance, seized my beard, and gave it a tug. ⁸'John,' he said, 'don't be skeptical but be a believer; and don't be so inquisitive.'ᵃ

⁹"I replied, 'What have I done, Lord?'

¹⁰"But I tell you, my fellow believers, that for a month I suffered so much pain in the spot where he touched my beard that I said to him, ¹¹'Lord, if your playful tug has caused so much discomfort, what if you had given me a slap or two?!'

¹²"He answered, 'From now on take care not to test the one who cannot be tested.'ᵃ

91 "By this time Peter and James were irked that I was speaking with the Lord; and they gestured that I should leave the Lord by himself and go back to them. ²I did so, and they both asked, 'Who was the old man speaking with the Lord on the mountain? We heard two people speaking.'

³"After considering his abundant grace, his oneness under many forms, and his wisdom that never turns its gaze from us, I said, 'If you ask him, you will get your answer.'

92 "Again, on a later occasion when all of his disciples were sleeping in the same house at Gennesaret, I, acting on my own, covered myself up in my cloak and tried to discover what he was doing. ²Right away he said, 'John, go to sleep.'

³"Then, while I was feigning sleep, I saw someone else like him and heard him say to my Lord, 'Jesus, those whom you have chosen continue not to believe in you.'

⁴"My Lord replied, 'You are right, for they are <mere> humans.'

93 "I shall describe another divine manifestation, brothers and sisters. ²At times I would find a material, solid body when I sought to touch him; but at other times I would grasp at an immaterial and incorporeal substance, just as if it were not there.

³"We would accompany him whenever he accepted a dinner invitation from a Pharisee.ᵃ ⁴Each of us, Jesus included, would receive from the hosts a normal-sized loaf of bread, but he would bless his

---

90:8 • *don't be skeptical but be a believer:* μὴ γίνου ἄπιστος ἀλλὰ πιστός, as in Jn 20:27.

93:1 • *divine manifestation:* δόξα, usually translated "glory," can refer to various aspects of divinity.

and distribute it among us. ⁵That small piece would fully satisfy each of us, and our individual loaves would be untouched, leaving our hosts astonished.

⁶"Often, while walking with him, I tried to see if he left a footprint in the ground; but, observing that he kept himself suspended above the earth, I never saw a footprint.

⁷"I share this much with you, fellow believers, so as to incite you to faith in him. ⁸For the present, a veil of silence must cloak his mighty deeds and wonders, since they are not to be named and possibly could not be spoken or understood.

94 "Prior to his arrest[a] by lawless Jews (whose 'laws' were given by the lawless serpent), the Lord assembled us all and said, ²ᵃ'Before I am delivered to those people[a] let us praise the Father in song and so go forth to what lies ahead.'

³ᵃ"He had us join hands and form a circle. Placing himself in the middle, he said, 'Respond to me with "Amen,"' and led off the song:

> ¹Glory to you, Father.
> > *Circling we sang the 'Amen.'*
> Glory to you, Word,
> Glory to you, Grace.
> > Amen.
> ²Glory to you, Spirit,
> Glory to you, Holy One,
> Glory to your Glory.
> > Amen.

94:1a ᵃCf. Mk 14:48; Mt 27:55; Lk 22:54; Jn 18:12; Acts 1:16
94:2a ᵃCf. Jn 18:36

93:6 • *I never saw a footprint:* There is a striking parallel in Philostratus *Heroicus* 13.2, where the Vinedresser narrates an encounter with an athletic spirit: "As he ran you could not see a footprint, nor did his foot make any mark upon the ground." Speculation about footprints may be traced back at least to exegesis of Homer *Iliad* 13.68-72 (the departure of Poseidon from his mission of encouragement in battle). Commenting on *Iliad.* 22.8, Clement of Alexandria (*Stromateis* 5.14) states that "the divinity cannot be captured by a mortal, or apprehended either with feet, or hands, or eyes, or by the body at all." Several early Christian writings stress the corporeality of the resurrected Jesus, e.g., Lk 24:39; Ignatius *Smyrnaeans* 3.2 "I am not a bodiless demon"; Ep apost 11.8 "The foot of a ghost or a demon does not join the ground."
94:1–102:3 • It is widely held that these chapters are a late addition to the writing; see the Introduction.
94:1 • *Circling ...:* Italics in AJn 94–96 denote rubrics, comments, or responses.
94:2a, 3a • These verse numbers have "a" affixed to them to preserve the conventional verse numbers of the hymn that follows.
94:2a • *let us praise ... in song,* literally, "let us sing a hymn" (ὑμνήσωμεν): cf. Mk 14:26; Mt 26:30.

94:3 ᵃCf. 1 Jn 1:5; Jas 1:17
95:13 ᵃCf. Mt 11:17; Lk 7:32

³We praise you, O Father,
We give thanks to you, O Light,
In whom darkness does not reside.ᵃ
  Amen.

95
Now I shall tell you why we give thanks:

⁴I wish to be saved and I wish to save.
  Amen.
⁵I wish to be freed and I wish to free.
  Amen.
⁶I wish to be wounded and I wish to wound.
  Amen.
⁷I wish to be born and I wish to beget.
  Amen.
⁸I wish to eat and I wish to be eaten.
  Amen.
⁹I wish to hear and I wish to be heard.
  Amen.
¹⁰I wish to be understood, as I am all understanding.
  Amen.
¹¹I wish to be washed and I wish to wash.
  Amen.
  Grace dances.
¹²I wish to pipe: all of you, dance.
  Amen.
¹³I wish to lament: all of you, beat your breasts.ᵃ
  Amen.
¹⁴The one Ogdoad sings in chorus with us.
  Amen.
¹⁵The Twelfth number dances on high.
  Amen.
¹⁶The entire universe is to dance on high.
  Amen.

94:3 • For the dance as a metaphor of the relation of humans to the One see Plotinus, *Enneads* 6.9.8.
95:14 • *Ogdoad*, "Eighth" (ὀγδοάς), untranslated here because of its importance in cosmology.
95:14 • In a thorough and mature Valentinian work one would expect a decad between vv. 14 and 15 to make the total of thirty entities in the *Pleroma*.
95:16 • *The entire universe ...*: Translation is difficult; more literally, "To the whole (universe) belongs dancing on high." This may mean that dancing is characteristic of the (heavenly) universe or that the one who dances has possession of that totality.

¹⁷Whoever does not dance is ignorant of what is taking
   place.
   Amen.
¹⁸I wish to take flight, and I wish to remain here.
   Amen.
¹⁹I want to adorn, and I want to be adorned.
   Amen.
²⁰I want to be united and I want to unite.
   Amen.
²¹I possess no house, yet I possess houses.[a]
   Amen.
²²I have no place, yet I have places.[a]
   Amen.
²³I have no temple, yet I have temples.[a]
   Amen.
²⁴I am a lamp to you who see me.
   Amen.
²⁵I am a mirror to you who perceive me.[a]
   Amen.
²⁶I am a door to you who knock upon me.[a]
   Amen.
²⁷I am a path to you, the wayfarer.[a]
   Amen.

96

²⁸In response
   to my dance,
²⁹see yourself
   in me as I speak.[a]
³⁰When you have seen what I do,
   keep my mysteries secret.
³¹You who dance,
   understand what I do, because
³²what I am about to endure is yours:
   it is the suffering of humankind.
³³You could not in any way
   understand what you suffer,

95:21 [a]Cf. Jn 14:2; Heb 3:6
95:22 [a]Cf. Mt 8:20; Lk 9:58
95:23 [a]Cf. 1 Cor 3:16–17; 2 Cor 6:16
95:25 [a]Cf. 96:29
95:26 [a]Cf. Jn 10:7, 9
95:27 [a]Cf. Jn 14:6
96:29 [a]Cf. 95:25

95:24 • *I am a lamp:* The use of this imagery is reminiscent of *Odes Sol.* 13.1; see also Rev 21:23.
95:24 • *to you:* From here to the end of the hymn "you" is singular.

> ³⁴if I had not been sent to you
>> as Word by the Father.
> ³⁵You who have seen what I suffer
>> have seen me as one who suffers;
> ³⁶and when you saw, you did not remain stationary,
>> but were shaken to your very roots.
> ³⁷You have me as a place of rest:
>> find rest in me.[a]
> ³⁸You will discover who I am
>> when I depart:
> ³⁹I am not
>> what I now appear to be.
> ⁴⁰You will see what I am
>> when you come.
> ⁴¹If you were to understand suffering,
>> you would have within your grasp the possibility of not suffering.
> ⁴²Learn what suffering is,
>> and you will possess the capacity to escape it.
> ⁴³I myself shall teach you
>> what you do not know.
> ⁴⁴I am your God,
>> not <the god> of the betrayer.
> ⁴⁵I want to make holy souls
>> share in my heavenly melody:
> ⁴⁶Learn the message of wisdom.
>> Say to me once more:
> ⁴⁷Glory to you, Father;
>> Glory to you, Word;
>> Glory to you, Spirit.
> ⁴⁸If you want to know my 'Amen,'
>> by word I once made light of all things,
>> and I was not put to shame at all.
> ⁴⁹Now that I have done my dance,
>> you, for your part,
>> come to understand the All;

96:37 [a] Cf. Mt 11:28

96:36 • *and when you saw ...*: The text of this passage is corrupt; a word or two may be missing.

96:34 C reads: "to you (sg.) I am word; I was sent by [the] father."

96:35 *what I suffer*: reading ὃ πάσχω with C against Junod-Kaestli "what I do" (ὃ πράσσω).

⁵⁰and, once you have understood it, say:
'Glory to you, Father. Amen.'

97 "After the Lord had finished this dance with us, beloved, he left <us>. ²We fled away in various directions, acting as if we were bewildered or drugged with sleep.ᵃ ³For my part, when I saw him suffering, I could not stand it but took refuge on the Mount of Olives, weeping at what had happened. ⁴When he was crucified at noon on Friday, darkness covered the whole earth.ᵃ

⁵"Then the Lord suddenly appeared in the cave <where I had secluded myself> and bathed me with radiance. ⁶'John,' he said, 'as far as the crowd below in Jerusalem is concerned I am hanging on the cross,ᵃ being pierced with lances and reedsᵇ and given vinegar and gall to drink.ᶜ ⁷In reality I am addressing you here: listen to what I have to say. ⁸I put it into your mind to come up this mountain so that you might hear what the pupil should learn from the teacher, the human from God.'

98 "He then showed me a Cross of Light firmly anchored, and around the cross a huge crowd. ²This crowd had no definite form; but on the cross there was a definite form, a corresponding pattern. ³I saw the Lord himself above the cross, with no bodily features, but only as a voice, and not the voice to which we were accustomed, but a gentle, comforting sound—without doubt the voice of God. ⁴The voice said, 'John, one person must hear what I have to say—I require a single individual to hear what is to come:

⁵"'For your sake I refer to the Cross of Light <in various ways>: as Word, or Mind, or Christ, or Door, or Way, or Bread, or Seed, or Resurrection, or Son, or Father, or Spirit, or Life, or Truth, or Faith, or Grace. ⁶These terms, indeed, are condescensions to human weakness.ᵃ ⁷Yet what it actually is, when comprehended on its own

97:2 ᵃCf. Mk 14:50; Mt 26:56; Jn 16:32
97:4 ᵃCf. Mk 15:33; Mt 27:45; Lk 23:44
97:6 ᵃCf. 99:2
ᵇCf. Jn 19:34
ᶜCf. Mk 15:36; Mt 27:34, 48; Jn 19:29
98:6 ᵃCf. 101:13

97:5 • To this highly docetic crucifixion account compare the close parallel in the *Second Treatise of the Great Seth*, NHC VII,2:55,30–56,19, translated by Roger A. Bullard and James A. Gibbons in James M. Robinson, ed., *The Nag Hammadi Library*, 363–71, 55.31–56.20, p. 365, and the comments of L. Painchaud, *Le deuxième traité du grand Seth*, 100–6. Cf. also Ovid *Fasti* 3.701–4, which reports that a phantom was substituted for the apparently executed Caesar, who was taken up into heaven.
98:3 • *saw ... as a voice* (τινα φωνὴν μόνον): cf. Rev 1:12; AJn 99:2; APl 3.7; ATh 27:3.
98:5 • <in various ways> stands for ποτέ ("sometimes"), repeated before each of the nouns that follow.
98:5 • *Word, or Mind, ...*: The titles given have in some cases a biblical precedent: Word (Jn 1:1); Mind (1 Cor 2:16); Christ (NT passim); Door (Jn 10:9); Way (Jn 14:6); Bread (Jn 6:35–48); Seed (Junod-Kaestli cite Mk 4:46; Lk 8:5, 11); Resurrection (Jn 11:25); Son (NT passim); Father; Spirit; Life (Jn 11:25; 14:6); Truth (Jn 14:6; Junod-Kaestli also cite Jn 1:14, 17); Faith; Grace (Junod-Kaestli cite Jn 1:14, 17).

98:9 [a]1 Cor 15:24; Eph 1:24; 6:12; Col 2:10, 15; AJn 98:9
[b]Cf. 36:4
99:2 [a]Cf. 97:6
[b] → 98:3
99:3 [a]Cf. Mk 8:27–28; Mt 13–14; Lk 9:18–19

terms and put into words for your benefit, is the proper distinction of all, the secure recovery of what is well-rooted from amidst what is uncertain; <in short,> the disposition of Wisdom.

[8]"'When Wisdom's disposition is present, those on the right <side> come to be—but also those on the left:[a] [9]authorities, principalities,[a] demons, forces, threats,[b] passions, accusations, Satan, and the lower root; from this last arises the nature of created entities.

99

"'This cross, then, which has anchored all by word and separated out what derives from creation and the inferior, and has then permeated all things, is not the wooden cross you will behold when you go down from this place. [2]Nor am I the one upon the cross,[a] I whom you do not see, but whose voice alone you hear.[b] [3]I was imagined to be what I am not, since I am not who the masses think I am.[a] [4]What they shall say about me is beneath me and unfitting to my station. [5]Since, then, the place of rest is beyond your powers of sight or speech, I, its Lord, am even more indescribable and ineffable.

100

"'The crowd without distinct form around the cross is the lower nature. [2]If not all those whom you saw on the cross have a single form, that is because not every member of the one who has come down has yet been gathered. [3]When, however, the essential reality of authentic humanity, the race which cleaves to me in obedience to my voice, is taken up to glory, those who hear me now will be together with that race, no longer as they are now, but above the cross—just as I am now above it. [4]For so long as you do not identify yourself as belonging to me, I am not that which I was. [5]But if you listen to me, you will be like me, and I shall be what I was [...]. [6]So take no thought for the masses, and treat with contempt those who

100:3 • Similarly, Clement of Alexandria, *Excerpts from Theodotus* 26.3.
100:6 • *all that I am ...*: This concluding phrase (με ὅλον παρὰ τῷ πατρὶ καὶ τὸν πατέρα παρ' ἐμοί) is strongly reminiscent of Jn 10:30; 14:11 (cf. 17:21), and is introduced with a verb of knowing (γίνωσκε) that likewise recalls Jn 10:38 (ἵνα γνῶτε καὶ γινώσκητε [v.1. πιστεύσητε]). AJn 100:6 adds the word ὅλον, which here may be taken either adjectivally (as in the present translation: "*all of me*") or adverbially ("I am in the Father *completely*"). This longer version of the saying occurs, probably independently, in Ep apost 17.4, and is quoted by later authors (e.g., Augustine *Serm.* 9).

98:8 Lallemann proposes to emend the text with a negative: "not present," *Acts of John*, 192. He does not justify this change on the grounds of textual criticism, but holds that it produces better sense.
100:5 *what I was ...*: The text is corrupt, in that there is a small lacuna.

do not share the mystery; know instead that all that I am is with the Father, and the Father with me.

101 "'This means that I suffered none of the things which they will claim. ²More than this, I intend that the suffering I revealed to you and the others in my dance be called a mystery. ³Now you see what you are: I have shown it to you; I alone know what I am: no one else knows. ⁴Let me have what is mine;ᵃ discover what is yours through me. ⁵I did not say that it is possible to see me as I really am, but to see what is within your capacity to grasp, because you are my kindred. ⁶You hear that I suffered: in fact, I did not; that I did not suffer when, in fact, I did. ⁷<You hear> that I was pierced: in fact, I was not injured; that I was crucified, when in fact, I was not. ⁸<You hear> that blood flowed from me,ᵃ when in fact, it did not. ⁹Very simply, I did not experience the things they say about me; but what they deny, those things I did experience. ¹⁰I am going to tell you what these are in enigmatic speech, because I know that you will understand: ¹¹Understand me, therefore, as

> the capture of the Word,
> > the piercing of the Word,
> the blood of the Word,
> > the wounding of the Word,
> ¹²the hanging of the Word,
> > the suffering of the Word,
> the nailing of the Word,
> the death of the Word.

¹³"'By speaking in this way I have accommodated human weaknesses.ᵃ ¹⁴First, understand "Word"; then you will understand "Lord"; and, thirdly, <you will understand> "human," and what he has suffered.'

102 "After he had said these things to me (and others that, in accordance with his will, I am not to speak), he was taken up,ᵃ although none of the crowd observed his ascension. ²On my way down <the mountain> I laughed at them all as they told me what they had to say about him, holding firmly within myself this tenet: ³the Lord had done all things symbolically and suitably for the conversion and salvation of the human race.

101:4 ᵃCf. ATh 100:4
101:8 ᵃCf. Jn 19:34
101:13 ᵃCf. 98:6
102:1 ᵃCf. Mk 16:19; Acts 1:2; GPet 19

103:1 ᵃCf. Acts 1:23; Gal 2:9
104:1 ᵃCf. Eph 1:21
104:3 ᵃCf. Mt 10:28

103 "Therefore, brothers and sisters, since we have glimpsed the graceᵃ of our Lord and his affection for us, let us who have become recipients of his mercy worship him, not with fingers, mouths, tongues, or any bodily organ, but with souls properly disposed [...]. ²Let us remain vigilant, because he is our companion for our sake, in prisons and tombs, in bonds and dungeons, in reproaches and insults, on sea and land, in beatings, condemnations, conspiracies, entrapments, and punishments. ³In brief, he himself is with all of us who suffer, and he shares our pangs. ⁴He cannot abide overlooking any of us who invoke him, brothers and sisters, but, as he is everywhere, he hears every one of us. ⁵At this time, as the God of us who are in prison, he has, of his own dear compassion, brought help to Drusiana and to me.

104 "Be convinced, therefore, beloved, that I am not proclaiming a human being for you to worship, but God unchangeable, God invincible, God above every authority and power,ᵃ ²more ancient and mighty than all angels and all so-called or imagined creatures and all spiritual beings. ³If you persevere in this belief and fortify yourselves with it, you will possess a soul that cannot be destroyed."ᵃ

105 After he had communicated this information to the believers, John went out for a walk with Andronikos. ²Drusiana and the faithful followed from afar—to see the mighty deeds done by him, to hear his message, and <to be> in the Lord always [...].

EPISODE 5

LACUNA III

AJn 105 is probably not a conclusion. Perhaps the two incidents found in fragmentary form in P. Oxy. 850 belong at this point (see below, Appendix A).

103:1 • *souls properly disposed ...:* The text is corrupt; the original may have been deleted for theological reasons.
105:1 • *communicated* (παραδούς) suggests not merely reporting data but handing on the tradition; cf. 1 Cor 11:2; 15:3.
105:2 • *in the Lord always:* A copyist has rounded off this passage with "Now and always, world without end. Amen," and may be responsible for the phrase "in the Lord always."

EPISODE 6

THE FALL OF THE HOUSE OF ARTEMIS

37 The Milesian believers said to John, "We have been in Ephesus for a long time. ²If it is acceptable to you, let us go to Smyrna—we understand that the mighty deeds of God have already become news there."

³Andronikos, however, said, "Let us not go there until the teacher wishes it."

⁴John, for his part, proposed <the following>: "Let us first visit the Temple of Artemis. Perhaps when we appear there the servants of the Lord will make themselves known."

38 Now, two days later the idolatrous temple kept its feast of dedication. ²Everyone but John was wearing festive white; he went up to the temple dressed in black—so they seized him and were bent upon putting him to death. ³But John said, "You are mad, my dear fellows, to lay violent hands upon me, a servant of the <one and> only God." ⁴Then he made his way to a high platform[a] and began to address them:

39 "Good people of Ephesus,[a] you are dangerously prone to behave like the ocean. ²Every disgorging river and each descending spring—the rains, the buffeting waves, and rock-filled torrents—all alike become bitterly saline from the seasoning effect of the sea. ³In the same way the corrupting effect of your ancient religious observance has up to this very day kept you immune to the force of authentic religion. ⁴Despite the vast number of marvels and healings that I have brought about and which you have seen, your hearts remain blind and you are incapable of sight. ⁵What else could I do, citizens of Ephesus,[a] but have the temerity to come up and enter this your idolatrous shrine? ⁶I shall prove to you, by the use of human reason, that you are utterly godless and effectively dead:

38:4 [a]Cf. ATh 37:2
39:1 [a] ⇢ 33:1
39:5 [a] ⇢ 33:1

37:2 • *the mighty deeds of God:* τὰ μεγαλεῖα τοῦ θεοῦ, as in Acts 2:11.
38:1 • *dedication:* ἡ γενέθλιος (sc. ἡμέρα, omitted as often) commonly refers to a birthday or anniversary; in Jn 10:22 the "Dedication" or "Festival of Lights" is τὰ ἐγκαίνια, "celebrations of renewal."

⁷"You see me standing here; all of you maintain that you consider Artemis a goddess. ⁸So, then, entreat her that I fall dead—just I. ⁹If you can't achieve this, I—just I—shall beseech my own God that I might put you all to death as punishment for your unbelief."

40 But they, who had had considerable experience of John and had seen the dead come to life, began to shout, "Don't destroy us in this way, we implore you, John! We know well that you can."

²"Well, then," he replied, "if you do not wish to die, this cult of yours must be condemned. Why? So that you may abandon your long-standing deception. ³The hour has come! Either convert to my God or let me be put to death by yours, for I shall pray here, in your presence, beseeching my God to have mercy on you."

41 Having said this, John uttered the following prayer: "O God, who are God above all who are called gods, who have until now been rejected by Ephesus, who gave me the idea of coming to this place—a notion I have never entertained; ²you who reprove all pagan piety through turning people to worship you, at whose name every idol and demon flees, as well as every power and impure being; ³now, therefore, by the power of your name, cause the demon that has deceived this vast multitude to flee—⁴yet show your mercy here in this place, because these people have been misled."

42 As John said all this the altar of Artemis suddenly shattered into fragments; all the dedicatory objects in the temple suddenly pitched to the ground; so, too, more than seven statues were split and their bows broken. ²A good half of the shrine collapsed, killing with one blow the priest, who was crushed in the crash by the main beam. ³So that crowd of Ephesians began to shout, "There is no god like John's God, the one God who shows us mercy, for you alone are

---

39:8 • *just I:* John's challenge is reminiscent of the contest between Yahweh and Baal initiated by Elijah in 1 Kgs 18:17–40 and Daniel's encounter with Bel's clergy: Dan 14:1–22 (Bel et Draco).
40:3 • *for I shall pray:* Junod-Kaestli leave the word "for" (γάρ) untranslated, beginning a new sentence with "I shall pray." But the sense seems to be this: though, in the mind of the crowd, Artemis may rage against John, he will not fight back; on the contrary, he shall pray for her worshipers (see 41:4).

42:1 *their bow(s):* This is based upon the conjecture of Junod-Kaestli (1. 222 n. 42): τόξον, as the bow is an attribute of Artemis the hunter. Some MSS read δόξαν "majesty," which they suspect was an attempted restoration of a corrupt or unintelligible word.

God. ⁴Now we have accepted conversion, we who have witnessed your marvels. ⁵Have mercy on us, O God, in accordance with your will, and deliver us from our great deception."

⁶Some prostrated themselves in supplication, while others knelt to pray; some wept and tore their garments, while others tried to run away.

43 With outstretched hands and heart uplifted, John praised God: "Glory to you, my Jesus, the only true God,ᵃ for you acquire your servants in many and various manners." ²To the crowd he said, "Get up off the ground, good people of Ephesus,ᵃ and pray to my God: acknowledge that invisible power of his that has been made manifestly apparent, and the wonderful deeds wrought before your very eyes. ³Artemis, after all, really ought to have come to her own aid; she should also have rescued her servant and not let him die. ⁴Where is the power of this demon? ⁵Where are the sacrifices, feasts of dedication, various solemnities, and sacrificial garlands, all offered in her honor? ⁶Where is all that potent magic and its sibling, sorcery?"

44 The people got up off the ground and quickly pulled down what was left of the idolatrous shrine, shouting as they did so, ²"The only God we recognize is the God of John; from now on we worship God, who has been merciful to us."

³As John was on his way out, an enormous crowd kept grasping him, crying, "Help us, John. Stand by us who are powerless and perishing. ⁴You see our determination; you see the crowd behind you clinging with hope in your God. ⁵We have come to see that we have been deceived into following a ruinous path. ⁶We have come to see that we set up our gods in vain; we have seen the shameful ridicule heaped upon them. ⁷Please allow us to come to your house and receive unhindered assistance. ⁸Take us in, for we have no remedy."

45 John answered, "My good people, please believe that I have remained in Ephesus for your sake—²although strongly inclined to

---

43:1 ᵃCf. 82:2
43:2 ᵃ ⇢ 33:1

43:1 • *only true God:* cf. *2 Clem.* 19:1; "only God": 1 Tim 1:17.
43:6 • *sibling* (ἀδελφή), literally, "sister," but the question of gender may be moot, since "sorcery" is a feminine noun (φαρμακία).
45:1 • *My good people* (Schäferdiek: "Friends") translates ἄνδρες (cf. Acts 14:15; 19:25; 27:10, 21, 25); see the note on 33:1 above.

45:3 ªCf. 87:3
46:2 ªCf. Jn 18:15
46:6 ªCf. Mt 8:22; Lk 9:60

go on to Smyrna and the other cities, so that Christ's servants in those places might also turn to him. ³But, since I would have left <this place> lacking full assurance about you, I have delayed my departure and prayed to God, imploring that I not leave Ephesus until I have made you strong in the faith.ª ⁴In view of what has taken place and, even more, of what is happening now, I am resolved not to leave you until I have weaned you, as children are weaned from their nurses' milk, and given you the solid stuff of a rock upon which to stand."

46 So John did not leave them, but received them at Andronikos' home. ²One of those who had gathered there happened to be a relativeª of the priest of Artemis. ³He had laid the priest's body down by the door and rushed in with the others, making no mention of this. ⁴John preached a homily to the crowd, led the prayers, offered the eucharist, and laid hands upon all present. ⁵This completed, he said, prompted from within, "Among those here is one who, impelled by faith in God, placed the body of the priest of Artemis outside the door before entering the house. ⁶Ardent for the salvation of his soul, he put concern for himself first, reasoning within himself, 'It's better to take thought for the living than to worry over my dead relative,ª ⁷for I'm quite sure that if I turn to the Lord and save my own soul, John will not refuse to raise up the dead also.'"

⁸John got up from his place and went over to the spot where the author of this reasoning, the priest's relative, had taken a place. ⁹Grasping his hand, John said, "Did you have these thoughts on your way in to see me, my child?"

¹⁰Shivering with fear, he confessed, "Yes, my lord," and hurled himself at John's feet.

¹¹The latter demurred: "Our Lord is Jesus Christ, who will demonstrate his power over your dead relative by raising him."

47 Lifting up the youth and continuing to grasp his hand, John said, "One who wields power over great mysteries has no difficulty

---

45:2 • *Christ's servants:* Those yet to be converted are already reckoned among the believers. Cf. Jn 4:35.
45:4 • For the various metaphorical elements here, see 1 Cor 3:1-2; Heb 5:14; Mt 7:24-27; Lk 6:47-49.

in taking up once more the lesser. Or is the healing of bodily illnesses a great matter? ²[... or is the driving out of demons living in the body a great matter? I know of other things greater than these, and I shall make known to you even others more amazing yet ...]." ³Still holding the youth's hand, John continued, "I say to you, my child, go yourself and raise up this corpse, using no other formula than these words, 'John, the servant of God, says to you: Arise.'"

⁴The youth, accompanied by a large crowd, went to his <dead> relative and spoke those very words; and he returned to John with the priest now alive.

⁵When John saw the one who had been raised, he said, "Despite the fact that you have risen, you are not truly alive now, nor are you an heir to or a participant in genuine life. ⁶Do you wish to belong to the one by whose name and might you have risen? Believe now and you will live forever."

⁷He immediately pledged his faith in the Lord Jesus and from then on kept close to John.[a]

47:7 [a]Cf. 54:5
48:5 [a]Cf. ATh 30:3

48 The next day John had a dream instructing him to walk three miles beyond the city gates. ²He did not ignore it but got up at dawn and set out upon the road, accompanied by the believers.

³Now there was at that time a local man whose father had been warning him to stop having sex with the wife of a coworker, who was threatening to kill the lad. ⁴Refusing to put up with this reprimand, the young man knocked his father down with a kick and left him lifeless. ⁵When John discovered this, he said to the Lord, "Lord, was this the reason you told me to come out here today?"[a]

49 Now when the young man saw this surprising death, he drew forth the sickle that was in his belt and set out on the run for

---

47:5 • *genuine life*, or "true life" (τὴν ἀληθινὴν ζωήν): Despite its apparent Johannine ring, the phrase does not appear in the gospel of John, where the preferred expression is "*eternal life*" (ἡ αἰώνιος ζωή).
48:1–2 • *had a dream*: For the same narrative device, see ATh 29:5.
48:3 • *a local man* (χωρικός), that is, someone born and bred in the vicinity; other translations, such as "countryman" (Schäferdiek) or "rural fellow," though defensible, either suggest that the man and John share a common homeland (Schäferdiek) or encourage ridicule of the rustic.

47:2 *... or is:* About three hundred letters in H are largely illegible. The bracketed text represents a partially conjectural restoration of a portion of the missing material.

his dwelling, expecting arrest. ²But John met him on the way, and commanded, "Halt, you shameless devil, and tell me where you are bound with that sickle so eager for blood?"

³The agitated youth let the tool fall to the ground and said, "I have done something dreadful and monstrous, and, knowing that I would be arrested, I have resolved to do myself an even more violent and savage wrong and then immediately die. ⁴My father constantly counseled me to live a temperate life, one free of adultery, but I couldn't stand his talk and gave him a kick that proved fatal. ⁵Seeing what had happened, I was on my way to the woman for whose sake I became a murderer, determined to do away with her, with her husband, and, last of all, with my own self. ⁶I couldn't tolerate letting the woman's husband see me receive the death penalty."

50 John responded: "Far be it from me to go off leaving someone to laugh at or mock you, or to overlook the danger facing you; so come along and show me where your father is lying. ²Now, if I raise him up for you, will you keep yourself away from the woman who has become so dangerous to you?"

³The youth agreed: "If you restore my father alive and I see him actually living and speaking, I will have nothing to do with her any longer."

51 As they were talking they came to the place where the old man lay dead, in the company of a number of passers-by who had stopped to loiter. ²John said to the youth, "You miserable creature, who wouldn't even spare your own father, old as he was!"

³The young man wept and tore at his hair and kept saying how much he regretted what he had done.

⁴John, the servant of God, then exclaimed: "You, <Lord,> who told me to come to this place today, who knew that this would result, you whom no earthly deed can elude; ⁵you who concede to me every kind of healing and remedy in accordance with your will: now, therefore, grant life to this elderly man. ⁶And since his killer has condemned himself, spare him, also, as you alone, O Lord, can do: spare him who spared not his father while he was engaged in the very act of giving his son excellent advice."

49:2 • *shameless devil* (δαίμων ἀναιδέστατε): The epithet or its equivalent appears also in AAnPas 49:3 (ὁ πάντα ἀναιδὴς διάβολος); ATh 33:2; 44:1; 74:4.

52 He thereupon approached the old man, saying, "The Lord will not hesitate to bestow his good mercy and unselfish beneficence[a] upon you. ²Get up, therefore, and glorify the work of God's hands."

³The old man said, "I am getting up, sir," and did so. ⁴He then sat down and lamented, "Just when I had been delivered from a dreadful life—in which I had to endure many grievous insults from a son who exhibited no filial concern—you have summoned me to return, you fine 'servant of the living god,' you! ⁵Kindly tell me why."

⁵[John replied, "If] you are rising to the very situation that you left, it would be better for you to remain dead. On the contrary, however, rise to better things." ⁶He took him and escorted him back to the city, proclaiming to him God's gracious message, so that before they had reached the gate the old man had become a believer.

53 When the young man had witnessed the unanticipated resurrection of his father and his own deliverance, he snatched his sickle and chopped off his genitals. ²He then scooped them up, rushed to the home of his mistress, threw them in front of her, and said, ³"Because of you I became my father's killer and would have killed you, your husband, and myself. ⁴Now you possess the semblance and source of this horror. ⁵<I was able to do all this> because God had mercy on me, so that I could know the divine power."

54 He had returned and told John, in the presence of the believers, what he had done.

²Now John responded to him: "The same one who led you to kill your father and to commit adultery with another's wife is the one who made you castrate yourself and reckon it a good deed. ³It was not the organs you needed to obliterate, but the thought they brought into the open: organs do not harm people but the unseen

---

52:6 • *gracious message* (χάρις), or simply "grace": In the NT, the noun is never found as the content of what is "proclaimed" (εὐαγγελίζεσθαι).
53:1 • *chopped off his genitals:* The young man follows the counsel of Mt 19:12; Origen, the author's near contemporary, is reported to have done the same (see Eusebius *Hist. eccl.* 6.8.2).
53:5 • *<I was able ... this>* translates γάρ ("*for* God had mercy"); the sentence explains both the donation of sexual organs and the young man's conversion.

52:5 *John replied, "If ...*: The restoration of the lacuna is that of Bonnet, followed by Junod-Kaestli.

54:5 ªCf. 47:7

sources that motivate and elicit every shameful impulse. ⁴So then, my child, if you repent of this fault and come to learn the wiles of Satan, you will have God to help you in all your spiritual needs."

⁵The youth then repented of his former sins in order to receive pardon by the goodness of God and set himself to living a tranquil existence; and he would not be separated from John.ª

55 While John was accomplishing these things at Ephesus, some Smyrnaeans dispatched representatives to him with this message: ²"We hear that you proclaim a god who is impartial and has commanded you not to give attention to one particular place. ³Since, then, you are the herald of such a god, come to Smyrna and the other cities so that we might come to know your god, and, knowing that god, there fix our hopes."

EPISODE 7

LACUNA IV

At this point the original Acts presumably described arrangements for the journey to Smyrna and, quite probably, other episodes in addition to that now found in AJn 56–57.

54:4 • *the wiles of Satan:* The thought parallels Eph 6:11.
55:2 • *impartial,* or "bountiful" (Schäferdiek): ἄφθονος, not found in the NT (but see ἀφθονία in Tit 2:7 v.l.), connotes both generosity (cf. Wis 7:13) and lack of prejudice.
55:2 • *one particular place:* The Smyrnaean representatives' concern recalls the earlier efforts of Kleobios and the wife of Marcellus to have John stay one day at Miletus (18:1).

EPISODE 8

ANTIPATROS RECOVERS HIS SONS

56 We left Ephesus and came to Smyrna.

²Learning that John had arrived, the whole populace assembled; and their leading citizen, a man named Antipatros, came up to John and said, "Servant of God, I have heard of the many and great wonders done by you at Ephesus. ³Here, I present you with 100,000 pieces of gold. <Why?> I have twin sons who have been plagued since birth by a demon; they are now thirty-four, and still suffer terribly. ⁴Both collapse at the same time, seized at the bath, or in the course of a walk or, often, at dinner or, sometimes, in the civic assembly. ⁵You will see for yourself that they are strapping fellows, but worn down by the malady which strikes them daily. ⁶Help me, I beseech you, old as I am: I am at the point of doing away with them. ⁷As infants they did not suffer too badly, but as grown men they have acquired even more potent and forward demons. Therefore, have mercy on me and on them."

⁸"My physician does not accept monetary payment," answered John, "but heals free of charge, accepting as payment the souls of those healed from their illnesses. ⁹What do you want, Antipatros, in exchange for your children? ¹⁰Offer to God your very soul and you will get back your children, made well by the power of Christ."

¹¹"Until now," replied Antipatros, "you've overlooked no one; don't begin with my two sons. ¹²With the consent of the entire family, I have decided to put them to death by poison to end the ridicule. ¹³But here you are, a trustworthy physician acting on God's behalf: Come to them, illumine them, help them."

57 In response to this request, John prayed to the Lord: "Constant consoler of the humble when invoked, who never waits to

---

56:1 • *We left Ephesus and came to Smyrna:* If the Acts of John originally contained more material at this point, this sentence is a summary by an epitomator or a copyist repairing a breech in the text.
56:1 • At this point Bonnet introduces, in what he numbers AJn 56–57, an episode about John and a partridge (see below, Appendix B).

be invoked because you are present in person before your aid is sought: ²let the unclean spirits be cast out of the sons of Antipatros."

³They left at once.

⁴John gave orders that the sons come to him; and when their father saw them safe and sound, he fell down and worshiped John. ⁵[He gave them instructions concerning the Father, the Son, and the Holy Spirit, and baptized them]. ⁶And after enjoining Antipatros to give money to the poor, he dismissed them, as they praised and blessed God.

EPISODE 9

LACUNA V

This includes one or more episodes narrating the balance of John's ministry at Smyrna and his work at Laodicea and, possibly, other cities. The list of companions in AJn 59 suggests that there are other Lacunas. One may conjecture that Aristoboula's conversion ran parallel to that of Drusiana, involving a confrontation with an initially recalcitrant spouse. (Aristobula's name appears in the catalogue of heroines from apocryphal acts in the *Manichaean Psalm-Book* [Allberry, p. 192, 29].) Aristippos, Xenophon, and, last but not least, "the chaste prostitute," were also most probably the subject of one or more episodes, the loss of which will disappoint devotees of the apocryphal acts.

Perhaps the incident to which the third *Pseudo-Titus* citation alludes belongs in this place (see below, Appendix A).

56:4 • For a similar case of demonic possession, see ATh 62–64.
57:5 • This Trinitarian formula is almost certainly a later composition, and the following sentence may also derive from a copyist who rounded off the original account with a pious conclusion. The original ending will presumably have begun with a rejection by John of the homage offered, as in AJn 46.
57:6 • On the gap between this and the following chapters, see the Introduction, above.

EPISODE 10

FROM LAODICEA TO EPHESUS FOR A SECOND VISIT

58 Although a good deal of time had passed without any of the believers being distressed by John, they were quite upset when he said, ²"Brothers and sisters, the time has come to go to Ephesus, for I have made an agreement with those who remained there that I would come back to keep them from slackening because of having to endure a long while with no one to strengthen them. ³Now you must all keep your mind fixed upon God, who will not abandon you."

⁴When they had heard from him that he was going to leave them, the believers broke into tears of despair. ⁵John said, "I may leave you, but Jesus Christ is always with you. ⁶If your love for him remains unsullied, you will have fellowship with him that cannot be disrupted, for he loves those who love him before their love can be expressed."

59 After this, he bade them farewell, leaving a good deal of money for distribution to the believers. ²They all wept and moaned as John set out for Ephesus. ³With him were those who had been his companions since leaving Ephesus: Andronikos and Drusiana, and, with their respective retinues, Lykomedes and Kleobios. ⁴A number of others followed, including Aristoboula, who had learned of her husband Tertullus' death while traveling, Aristippos, Xenophon, and the chaste prostitute. ⁵John constantly urged them all to follow the Lord Jesus Christ. None of them would be separated from him.

60 The first day we[a] stopped at a lonely inn. ²Because we needed to find a bed for the blessed John to rest in, we saw a delightful

60:1 [a]Cf. ATh 1:2

58:1 • *From Laodicea ...:* This subheading is a later addition.
59:4 • *traveling* (ἐν τῇ ὁδῷ), literally, "on the way / road," possibly a double entendre including the "Way" of faith; cf. Mk 10:52; Acts 19:9.
60:1 • *The first day ...:* The vocabulary, style, and form of AJn 60–61 strongly suggest that this is, at least in its current recension, a later stratum of the tradition. In late antiquity animal stories were popular means for expressing philosophical or religious views. For other examples, see ATh 30–41, 68–81. Pythagoreans and rabbis were among those who employed this device. See, in general, Spittler, *Animals*; on this episode in particular, 96–110. Form-critically this is an extended pronouncement story.

incident involving him. ³There was one unmade bed lying about someplace in the room. ⁴We put upon it the cloaks we were wearing and urged him to lie down on it and get some sleep while the rest of us bedded down on the floor. ⁴Once he had lain down, however, John was aggravated by a huge number of bugs; <and> they became ever more vexatious. ⁵Around the middle of the night we all heard him address them, ⁶"I say to you, bugs, you must behave yourselves, one and all. Leave your home at once and settle quietly in a single spot, and keep your distance from the servants of God." ⁷As we chuckled and continued to talk, John went to sleep. We spoke softly so as not to disturb him.

61 Along with Verus and Andronikos I was first to rise at dawn. We saw a large band of bugs by the door of our room. ²The sight was astonishing, and everyone else got up to see the insects. John, however, slept on. ³After he had been awakened, we told him what we had seen. ⁴He then sat up in bed, looked at the bugs ... and said, "Since you have been decorous and have paid heed to my rebuke, you may return to your place." ⁵He then got out of bed. ⁶The bugs scampered across the room to the cot, swarmed up its legs, and ensconced themselves within the framework. ⁵John spoke up once more: "This created species was obedient to the voice of a human being, keeping quietly off by itself without transgressing, but we, who hear the voice of God, are lax and disobedient. How long can this continue?"

62 Later, when we got to Ephesus, the believers there learned that John had returned after a long absence and thronged together at Andronikos' house, where John lodged. ²They grasped his feet, pulled his hands to their faces and kissed them; they even kissed their own hands that had reached out to grasp him simply because those hands had touched his clothes.

61:4 *looked at the bugs:* Ca. twenty letters in H are illegible here.

EPISODE 11

DRUSIANA AND KALLIMACHOS
A Life and Death Adventure

63 While the community was basking in abundant love and unsurpassable joy, a certain individual, launched on his course by Satan, saw Drusiana and lusted after her, although he knew well that she was Andronikos' wife. ²Any number of people told him, "There is no way for you to get this woman. She has long since ceased marital relations with her husband on the grounds of piety. ³Are you alone ignorant of how Andronikos—he has not always been the devout fellow he now is—enclosed her in a tomb, asserting, 'Either be to me the wife you once were, or die'? ⁴In fact, she preferred to die, preferred death to sharing his considerable wealth, preferred to be put to death rather than to do that hateful deed. ⁵If, then, she would not have sex with her lawful husband and master but even persuaded him to adopt her viewpoint, do you imagine that she will consent to commit adultery with you? ⁶Renounce this obsession that gives you no respite. Renounce this project that you cannot accomplish. ⁷Why continue adding fuel to the flame of your desire by imagining that you can gratify it by your brashness?"

64 Despite such words, his intimate friends could not convince him; on the contrary, he had the impudence to send her a message! ²Eventually, however, he despaired of his plans for her and, in order to avoid continued rebuffs, desisted. He lapsed into listlessness. ³Now, two days later Drusiana took to her bed with a fever caused by his malaise. ⁴"Would that I had never returned to my native city," she lamented, "and become a source of temptation to a man uninitiated in religious duties. ⁵If only he had instead been smitten with the message, he would not have fallen into such a wretched state. ⁶Therefore, Lord, since I share responsibility for this injury to an uninformed soul, release me from these bonds and take me to you at once." ⁷So, while John was present [in Ephesus], Drusiana departed this life, but he knew nothing about the matter. ⁸She did not die happy, but in grief over the man's damaged soul.

63:3 • *Either be to me ...:* This is an explicit reference to the Lacuna that preceded AJn 87.

65 Andronikos, secretly troubled, lamented both silently and with open tears, so that John would often silence him, saying, ²"Drusiana has passed on to a better hope, having left this unjust life behind."

³Andronikos had this answer: "I am sure of it, [Father] John, and I know that I have no doubt whatsoever about my faith in God. ⁴Most of all, I cling to this conviction, that she died in a state of purity."

66 When, however, she had been buried and John had consulted Andronikos and learned what had caused her death, he became more unhappy than Andronikos. ²He sat in silence for a brief period, puzzled over the outrages of the Adversary. ³Then, after all the believers had assembled to hear what he would say about the departed sister, he began to speak:

67 "A ship's captain must first bring the ship and those on board to a quiet and sheltered port before anyone may call the voyage safely completed. ²The farmer who has committed seeds to earth and labored mightily for their protection and nurture must first gather his abundant harvest into granaries before he may rest from his travail. ³The contestant engaged in a footrace must first obtain the prize before celebrating. ⁴The boxer entered in a match must first receive the crown before he begins to exult. ⁵Thus [it is] with all the other contests and pursuits: they are acknowledged only after they prove not fruitless in the end but are able to accomplish what they promised.

68 "I think that the same principle applies to the discipline of faith we each practice: it can be judged authentic if it persists at the same intensity right up to the time of death. ²Our minds let many obstacles creep in and cause trouble: anxiety, children, parents, repute, poverty, flattery, the prime of life, good looks, vanity, desire, wealth, anger, presumption, laziness, envy, jealousy, negligence, violence, lust, deceit, money, pretense, and all other obstacles of this sort. ³In the same way ship captains set on an easy voyage are opposed by hostile winds and a huge storm with great waves out of the blue, and the farmer by early frost, mildew, and vermin spring-

---

65:3 • *Father* is probably a later addition; see also 81:2.
67:5 • *Thus [it is]* ...: This is a difficult passage, possibly corrupt.

ing up from the earth, and the athlete by the 'almost good enough,' and those who practice a trade by the 'I could have done a little better.'ᵃ

69 "The believer must consider the end before everything else, and learn how to meet it, whether vigilantly, soberly, and without obstruction, or in a state of agitation, occupied with the cultivation of worldly affairs, and entrapped by desires. ²Similarly, one can praise the body only when it is altogether naked, call a general great only when the full object of the war has been achieved, call that physician superb only when every cure has been accomplished, and call a soul full of faith and worthy of God only when it has shown itself equal to its potential. ³One cannot commend a soul which began well but then slipped down into worldliness and fell, nor can one commend the sluggish soul which struggles to be involved with the higher things but is later dragged down into the transitory, ⁴nor that which longed more for the temporal than for the eternal, nor that which exchanged the enduring for the impermanent, ⁵nor that which values the valueless, nor that which honors what is to be rebuked, ⁶nor that which takes pledges from Satan, nor that which entertains the Serpent within its own bodily dwelling, ⁷nor that which makes fun of what is not to be mocked, nor that which is reviled for God's sake but is then ashamed, nor that which says 'yes' with the mouth but does not manifest that yes in deed. ⁸No. We must extol the soul that has the endurance not to be melted by filthy pleasure, nor to be overcome by indolence, nor to be lured astray by love of money, nor to be betrayed by sexual vigor or anger."

70 While John continued to address the believers at some length so as to teach them to hold the transitory in contempt, the man who had been enamored of Drusiana, his passion stoked by dreadful lust and the machination of the multiformed Satan, bribed Andronikos' chief servant (a greedy fellow) with a healthy sum. ²The servant opened Drusiana's tomb and thus provided him with the opportunity to subject her body to the unspeakable. (³Although unsuccessful while she was still living, he still longed for her body after death.) ⁴These were his words: "Since you would not have sex with me while you were alive, now that you are gone I shall violate you while you are defunct." ⁵After arranging this impious congress with the help of that foul head servant, he raced with him into the tomb, bent upon his resolution. ⁶They opened the door and fell to

68:3 ᵃ → 34:3

71:1 ᵃCf. ATh 31:1
73:2 ᵃCf. ATh 36:15; 80:12; 149:3; 160:5

ripping off the grave cloths from the corpse, saying, "What good did it do you, poor Drusiana? ⁷Couldn't you have done this while living? Had you done it wittingly, it just might not have been all that unpleasant."

71 When but a single wrap guarded her nudity, a snake suddenly appeared from somewhere,ᵃ struck at the servant and killed him with a single bite. ²It did not, however, smite the youth but wound itself around his feet, hissing fearfully. ³He collapsed, and the snake climbed upon him and lay there!

72 The next day, two days following Drusiana's death, John went to the tomb at dawn, along with Andronikos and the believers so that we might break bread there. ²When, despite a search that had begun at the outset, the keys could not be located, John said to Andronikos, "They are quite likely lost because Drusiana is not in the tomb. ³Nonetheless, let us go ahead so that you may not lapse. ⁴The doors will open on their own, just as the Lord has provided many other things for us."

73 When we reached the tomb, the doors came open at John's command, and they saw an attractive, smiling youth by Drusiana's grave. ²When John saw him he cried out, "Have you preceded us here also, O beautiful one?ᵃ Why?"

³He heard a voice say to him, "Because of Drusiana, whom I am now going to raise up. ⁴I have brought her within my realm for but a short while—and for the sake of the one who has expired next to her grave."

⁵After saying this the beautiful one ascended into the heavens as we looked on.

⁶John then turned his attention to the other side of the sepulcher and saw a young man, Kallimachos, a prominent Ephesian, with a huge serpent sleeping upon him, and the dead body of Andronikos' chief servant, Fortunatus. ⁷When he saw the two, he stood there perplexed and asked the believers, ⁸"What does this remarkable sight mean? Why did not my Lord, who has never been neglectful of me, make known to me what has happened in this place?"

72:1 • *we might break bread:* The first person plural ("we") appears abruptly here. See, e.g., 19:1; 94:1; 56:1.

74 When Andronikos saw the bodies he sprang forward into Drusiana's grave and, seeing her clad in nothing but a single wrap, said, "I know what has happened, John, blessed servant of God. ²Kallimachos here had a passion for my sister. ³Despite many unsuccessful, impudent advances, he gave this accursed chief servant of mine a large bribe, probably thinking, as we may conclude, that with his aid he could perform the melodrama he had plotted. ⁴Kallimachos had sworn to many people, 'If she will not consent to me while alive, she will be violated when dead.' ⁵So perhaps, John, the beautiful one determined that these remains would not be violated, and this is why those who essayed the outrage are dead. ⁶Was this not presaged by the voice which said to you, 'Raise up Drusiana—I have made her my intimate for but a short while'? ⁷Consider also that she died despondent, believing that she had become a source of temptation; <instead,> I believe the one who said that Kallimachos belonged to those who have been led astray, for you were commanded to raise her up. ⁸As for the other one, I know that he does not merit salvation. ⁹I do have one thing to ask from you: raise up Kallimachos first, and he will confess what has come to pass."

75 John cast his eyes upon the corpse and commanded the poisonous serpent, "Get away from the one who is about to become a servant of Jesus Christ." ²He then offered this prayer, standing: "God, whose name we rightly glorify, God who has mastery over every baneful force, God whose will is accomplished, who responds to us always, let the free gift of your grace be now accomplished in this youth. ³If any aspect of your plan for salvation is to come to pass through him, make it known to us when he is risen." ⁴The youth rose immediately, but remained silent for some time.

76 After he had recovered his senses, John asked him what his entry into the sepulcher meant. ²When he had learned from him just what Andronikos had proposed—that Kallimachos had indeed been enamored of Drusiana—John posed another question: ³"Surely you did not accomplish this foul plot and violate such chaste remains, did you?"

⁴He answered, "How could I, when this frightful creature struck down Fortunatus before my very eyes and with a single bite—quite justly, too, since he urged me on to the enormous madness after my passion had already cooled? ⁵The manner of his demise froze me with fear and put me in the state you saw before raising me. ⁶I shall

tell you something even more astonishing, something which really did me in and made me a corpse: ⁷After I, insane and disturbed by irresistible illness, had torn off the wrappings in which she had been entombed and had left the tomb and placed them carefully, as you can see, I went back to my unmentionable task and found an attractive young man shielding her with his cloak. ⁸Rays of light leapt from his face onto hers. He also made this statement to me: 'Kallimachos, die that you might live!'

⁹"I did not then know who he was, servant of God, but now that you have appeared here I recognize that he is a messenger of God, and I know full well and am convinced that the God you proclaim is true. ¹⁰Please, I implore you, do not stint to free me from this calamity and frightfully reckless enterprise. Present to your God an individual seduced by a foul and shameful deceit. ¹¹Would that you could tear open my chest to bring my thoughts to light! ¹²Henceforth a grievous burden lies upon my soul because I once thought the impermissible, and I have laid up for myself momentous grief because I succumbed to a dire temptation. ¹³I cleave to your feet, in need of your aid. I require your help to become good, like you, since otherwise I cannot belong to God. ¹⁴Nothing but this thought occupies my mind any longer: to have confidence in your God as a true and genuine son. ¹⁵I entreat you, as I wish to become one of those who hope in Christ, so that the voice which said to me in this place, 'Die that you might live,' may prove true. ¹⁶Its action has already been fulfilled, for that faithless, reckless, and godless one has died, and by you I have been raised, <I> who will be faithful, who will be devout, and who is to make the truth known. ¹⁷I beseech you to make this truth known to me."

77 John was overcome with great joy and, after reflecting upon the entire panorama of human salvation, said, ²"I do not know, Lord Jesus Christ, the extent of your power, being unable to comprehend the breadth of your compassion and the boundlessness of your patience. ³O what majesty has descended to the realm of servitude! What inexpressible nobility has been reduced to captivity! What incomprehensible glory—and our helper! ⁴You are king alone, made subject for us, you who kept this dead habitat free of outrage, who repudiated this young man's total lack of control over his sexual impulses and did not permit them to attain their object, ⁵who muzzled the raging demon within him and have shown mercy on one who had lost his mind, who are redeemer of one who had covered himself with gore, and reformer of one who had been buried, ⁶you who have not sent back the one who dissipated his fortune, nor turned your face from the one who repented. ⁷You are the father who has mercy and pity on one so neglectful of self. ⁸We glorify you; we praise, bless, and give thanks for your great goodness and mercy, holy Jesus, for you alone are God and no other. ⁹Yours is the power against which every machination is vain, both now and for all the ages, forever, amen."

78 After this prayer John put his arms upon Kallimachos, kissed him, and said, ²"Glory to our God, my son, to Christ Jesus, who has had mercy upon you and deemed me worthy to glorify his power; ³and has deigned also, by his own means, to turn you away from that madness and frenzy of yours, and has called you to find in him rest and newness of life."

79 When Andronikos saw Kallimachos raised from the dead and come to the faith, he, along with the sisters and brothers, begged John that he might raise Drusiana also, saying, ²"John, let Drusiana rise and make good that brief period during which she was dead in her distress over Kallimachos, supposing that she had become a source of temptation to him. ³The Lord will take her when he wills."

⁴John did not delay, but went to her grave and, taking Drusiana's hand, said, "I call upon you who alone are God, the most mighty, the ineffable, the unceasing, ⁵to whom every ruling power is subject, to whom all authority defers, to whom all arrogance bows in abject quietude, ⁶before whom all haughtiness falls down in silence, at whose voice demons tremble, ⁷in recognition of whom all creation stays within its bounds, whom flesh does not know, and of whom blood is ignorant. ⁸Let your name be glorified by us. ⁹Raise up Drusiana, so that Kallimachos may become stronger in you, who provide salvation and resurrection, gifts beyond human attainment and potential, but possible for you alone. ¹⁰Grant also that Drusiana may now find rest, since, with the conversion of the young man, she will have not even the slightest impediment upon her in her swift progress toward you."

80 After this prayer John said, "Drusiana, arise"; and then and there she rose and left the grave. ²When she realized that she was wearing only a shift, she was perplexed about her situation. ³While John lay prostrate in prayer and Kallimachos praised God in loud exclamations and frequent tears,ᵃ Drusiana learned in full detail from Andronikos what had happened, at which she also rejoiced and likewise added her own praise.

80:3 ªCf. Heb 5:7

81 After she had dressed, she glanced over and saw Fortunatus lying there. ²"Father," she said to John, "let him rise also, even if he tried to betray me in the worst possible way."

³When Kallimachos overheard this, he protested, "No, please, Drusiana, for the voice that I heard expressed no concern for him but spoke of you only. I witnessed it and I trust in it. ⁴If he had been good, God would presumably have had mercy upon him and raised him through the blessed John. ⁵The voice obviously implied that this fellow had come to a wicked end."

⁶John rebuked him: "My son, we did not learn to render evil for evil, for God has not given us a fair recompense for the many wicked and altogether bad things we have done to God, but repentance. ⁷Even when we didn't know the Name, God did not neglect us, but pitied us. When we blasphemed, God showed not vengeance, but compassion. ⁸Even when we did not believe, God bore no grudge. Even when we persecuted God's people, God did not reply in kind. ⁹Even when we dared to do unacceptable and frightening things, God didn't rebuff us, but urged us to repentance and avoidance of wickedness, and invited us toward the divine, as has happened for you, Kallimachos. ¹⁰Though you were unmindful of what had gone on before, God has made you a servant to minister by divine mercy. ¹¹Therefore, if you do not allow me to raise up Fortunatus, Drusiana will have to do it."

82 With exultant spirit and joyful soul she went unhesitatingly to the body of Fortunatus and offered this prayer:

>²Jesus Christ, God of the ages, God of truth,ᵃ
>>who have granted me to see signs and wonders,
>>who have graciously made me a sharer of your name,
>
>³who have manifested yourself to me in your multiform
>>countenance,
>>and have shown mercy in every fashion,
>
>⁴who protected me by your great goodness
>>when I was threatened with rape by my former consort,
>>>Andronikos,
>
>⁵who have given me Andronikos your servant as my brother,
>>who have kept me pure as your servant up to this very
>>>moment,

81:2 • *Father* is probably a later addition; see also 65:2.
82:2 • This is an excellent example of AJn's absolute identification of Christ as the one God.

82:2 ᵃCf. 43:1

⁶who raised me up when I had died, through John, your minister,
who, after I had risen, showed me the one
who had been overcome by temptation now no longer subject to it,
⁷who have given me perfect rest in you and have removed from me
the burden of secret madness—you whom I have cherished and loved—
⁸I beseech you, Jesus Christ, do not turn away your own Drusiana who begs you to raise up Fortunatus,
although he attempted to betray me in the worst way.

83 Taking the dead man by the hand, she said, "Rise, Fortunatus, in the name of Jesus Christ our Lord, even though you have been the bitterest enemy of her who serves God." ²Fortunatus then rose, but, when he saw John and Andronikos in the sepulcher, Drusiana risen from the dead, Kallimachos come to the faith, and the other believers all praising God, he cried, ³"Is there no limit to the powers of these dreadful people? I had no wish to be raised; I would rather be dead so that I would not have to see them." ⁴With these words he left the tomb and fled.

84 John, seeing that the soul of Fortunatus was incorrigible, exclaimed:

What a nature, unsuited by nature for improvement!
What a well of a soul bent upon living in sewage!
²What an essence of corruption full of darkness!
What a death, dancing with his own kind!
³What a fruitless tree, filled with fire!
What a trunk, with a demon for a mind!
⁴What a tree, producing charred wood for fruit!
What a forest, saddled with material madness and next door to unbelief!
⁵You have convinced us of your identity.
You are convicted forever, with your progeny.

82:6 In place of this verse, H has a partly legible text that may be reconstructed as follows (Junod-Kaestli 1.286):
Who, when I was dying, took me to yourself because of my grief; who said to me when I had left my body, "Drusiana, you are to be mine for a short while"; who have given John grace to raise me so that I might fulfill the brief course of my life; who showed me the one who had been overcome....

⁶You do not know how to praise what is superior,
    for you lack the very capacity;
⁷therefore, the path you follow
    is just like its root and nature.
⁸Have nothing to do with those
    whose hope is with the Lord—
⁹with their thoughts, with their mind,
    with their souls, with their bodies,
¹⁰with their practice, with their life,
    with their conduct, with their organization,
¹¹with their occupations, with their council,
    with their risen life in God,
¹²with their fragrance,
    in which you do not care to bask;
¹³with their fastings, with their prayers,
    with their holy bath, with their eucharist,
¹⁴with their bodily nourishment, with their drink,
    with their clothing, with their charity,
¹⁵with their burials of their dead,
    with their celibacy, with their righteousness.
¹⁶From all these, unholiest Satan, enemy of God,
    Jesus Christ will exclude you
    and all of your ilk who share your orientation.

85 After this, John prayed, took bread, and carried it into the sepulcher to break, offering this eucharistic prayer:
²We praise your name, which has turned us from error and
    merciless deception;
    we praise you who have made evident to our eyes what
    we have seen.
³We testify to your goodness displayed in manifold ways;
    we laud your good name, Lord, which has convicted
        those convicted by you.
⁴We give thanks to you, Lord Jesus Christ,
    because we are confident that <your grace> is invariable.
⁵We give thanks to you,
    because you require a saved nature.

84:13 • *with their holy bath* (λουτρόν): This term for baptism appears in Eph 5:26; Tit 3:5; APl 4.15.
85:4 • *<your grace>:* Bonnet proposes this reading for a missing noun phrase.

⁶We give thanks to you who have bestowed upon us the
    unshakable conviction
  that you alone are God, now and always.
⁷We your servants, gathered and assembled in good intent,
  give thanks to you, O holy one.

86
After he had thus prayed and offered praise, John distributed the Lord's eucharist to all the believers and then left the sepulcher. ²Once back at Andronikos' home, he said to the believers, "Sisters and brothers, a spirit within me has forecast that Fortunatus is going to die from the morbidity caused by the serpent's bite. ³Someone must go right now and discover if this is, in fact, the case."

³One of the young people ran out and found his remains putrefying, with the morbid decay spread about and extending even to his heart. ⁴The young person came back and reported to John that he had been dead for three hours.

⁵"Devil," said John, "you have got your offspring."ᵃ

86:5 ᵃCf. Jn 8:44; AAnPas 21:4; 40:2; 49:3

EPISODE 12

THE FAREWELL AND DEATH OF JOHN

106:2 ᵃCf. Rev 1:10; AAnPas 13:2; AJn 106:2; APt 29:4; 30:1; ATh 29:4; 31:9

106 The blessed John then passed some time with the believers, rejoicing in the Lord. ²The next day was the Lord's day,ᵃ and all the faithful had assembled.

³He began to speak: "Sisters and brothers, who together with me are servants, heirs, and participants in the dominion of the Lord— ⁴you are acquainted with God and the myriads of marvels God has granted you through me, and the vast host of signs, wonders, healings, spiritual gifts, teachings, directions, spiritual refreshments, services, occasions for praise, demonstrations of faith, sharing of goods, instances of grace, and gifts. ⁵All these you have seen before your faces, given by God, invisible as they are to earthly eyes and inaudible to earthly ears.

⁶"Therefore, strengthen yourselves in God, being mindful of God in all that you do, since you know why the Lord has performed the mystery of dispensation wrought for the salvation of humankind. ⁷The Lord in person begs and implores you through me, brothers and sisters. ⁸Christ, too, would remain free of distress and insult, treachery and punishment, for Jesus also is acquainted with dishonor, also familiar with treachery; ⁹and the Lord, too, knows punishment when you disobey the holy commandments.

107 Let not your good God be grieved,
    God the compassionate, the merciful, the holy, the
        pure,
    the undefiled, the immaterial, the only, the one,
    the unchanging, the sincere, the guileless, the
        unprovocable;
²the one higher and loftier than every attribute
    that can be named or imagined,
    the God Jesus Christ.

106:1 • The chapters traditionally enumerated AJn 87–105 are to be found above, following AJn 36.
106:2 • *the Lord's day*, that is, Sunday, as commonly in ECL.

³Let God rejoice with you
　　when you order your lives nobly.
⁴Let God share your merriment
　　when you act purely.
⁵Let God share your contentment
　　when you behave with dignity.
⁶Let God share your tranquility
　　when you lead celibate lives.
⁷Let God share your pleasure
　　when you share your goods.
⁸Let God share your laughter
　　when you practice self-denial.
⁹Let God experience delight
　　because of your love for God.

¹⁰"I am giving you this message, sisters and brothers, because I am now hastening to the task that lies before me, a task already being fulfilled by the Lord. What more might I say to you? ¹¹You possess the pledges of your God. ¹²You have the down payments of God's munificence. You possess God's unimpeachable presence. ¹³Therefore, if you sin no more, God forgives you what you have done in ignorance. ¹⁴But if you have known God and benefited from God's mercy, yet then return to your old ways, your former sins will be reckoned against you, and you will have neither share nor mercy in God's presence."

108 John then prayed:

Jesus, <you> who have fashioned this crown with your own weaving,
　　who have arranged these numerous blooms into your imperishable bouquet;
²who have sown your sayings like seeds,
　　you who are the sole protector of your servants
　　and the only physician who heals without charge;[a]
³the sole benefactor and only ruler who displays no arrogance,
　　the only source of mercy and generosity;
⁴the only savior and righteous one,
　　who are forever and in all and present everywhere;
⁵who encompass all things and fill all things,[a]
　　God and Lord Jesus Christ:

108:2 ᵃ → 22:3
108:5 ᵃCf. Col 1:15–20

⁶Shield with your free gifts and mercy all those who hope in you,
> you who know in full detail the schemes and outrages
> by which our ever-present adversary promotes intrigues against us.

⁷You, and you alone, O Lord,
> visit and assist your servants.

109 He then requested bread and prayed this eucharistic prayer:

²What doxology, oblation, or thanksgiving can we who break this bread
> pronounce other than you alone, O Jesus?

³We praise your name of Father, spoken by you;
> we praise your name of Son, spoken by you;

⁴We praise you as access to the door;
> we praise you as the resurrection made known to us through you.

⁵We praise you as way;
> we praise you as seed, as word, as grace, as faith,
> as salt, as pearl beyond description, as treasure, as plow,
> as net, as majesty, as diadem, as the one called for our sake Son of Man,
> as truth, as rest, as knowledge, as power, as commandment,
> as boldness, as freedom, as refuge found in yourself.

⁶You, O Lord, are the root of immortality, the source of incorruptibility,
> and the foundation of eternity.[a]

⁷You are designated with all these titles for our sake,
> so that by invoking you through them we might come to know your majesty—

⁸a majesty that cannot be seen by us in so far as we belong to the present world,
> but can only be perceived by the pure
> as they are shaped into the image of your unique person.

109:6 [a] Cf. Wis 15:3

109:1 • This chapter is theologically distinct, and as such quite likely a later addition; it may be compared to AJn 98 and contrasted with AJn 108.
109:3 • There are numerous variants for the two phrases preceding, most of which show interest in conformity to later Trinitarian formulations.

110 Then he broke the bread, and distributed it to us, *praying for each believer that he or she would be worthy of the Lord's grace and of the most holy eucharist.* ²He also partook and said, "May I also have a share with you," and "Peace,ᵃ beloved."

³John then said to Verus, "Get two believers with baskets and shovels and follow me."

⁴Verus did without delay that which John the servant of God had directed.

111 Setting out from the house, the blessed John passed beyond the city gates. ²He had instructed the majority of the believers not to accompany him. ³When he had reached the tomb of one of our own, he told the youths, "Dig here, my dear children."

⁴They began to dig.

⁵He kept urging them on vigorously, saying, "The trench must be deeper."

⁶As they dug, he preached to them and exhorted those who had come with him from the house, edifying them and fortifying them to grow toward the majesty of God, and offering a prayer for each one of us.

⁷When the youths had excavated to the desired depth and size—John alone understood; certainly none of us understood anything—he removed his outer garments and laid them like bedding at the bottom of the ditch. ⁸Clad only in his undergarment, he extended his hands in prayer:

112 You who have chosen us for a mission to the Gentiles, God,
     you who have sent us out into the whole world,ᵃ

110:2 ᵃCf. 115:2; Jn 20:19, 21, 26; AAnMt 3:5; 4:8; ATh 27:2; 70:4
112:1 ᵃCf. Gal 2:8

110:1 • *Then he broke the bread ...:* Since the apostolic death-stories enjoyed regular liturgical use, they were subject to regular revision in accordance with the dictates of theology and pious practice. AJn 110-115 have probably been contaminated by such change. Several MSS provide an expanded account in which John ordains Verus/Birros (probably to be identified with the Eutychos of Acts 20:7-12) deacon or metropolitan bishop and delivers a traditional charge. The words in italics are almost certainly later additions.
Junod-Kaestli 1.317-43 print three separate forms of the *Metastasis*, as the farewell scene is known.
110:2 • Bonnet (*Aaa* 2/1.209) begins AJn 111 at this point.
111:6 • *offering a prayer ...:* This phrase may have been the basis for the suspected interpolation in 110:1 (see note above).
112:1-9 • *You who have chosen ...:* The difference in content and theology from much of the rest of the *Acts of John* raises the suspicion that this prayer is a later reworking of or replacement for the original text.

113:1 ᵃCf. ATh 144:9

²who have revealed yourself through your apostles;
> you who never rest but ever save those who can be saved;

³who make yourself known throughout all nature,
> you who proclaim yourself even among the animals;

⁴who have made the savage and beastly soul civilized and tame,
> you who have given yourself to the soul thirsting for your words;

⁵who have hastened to appear to it when it was on the point of death,
> you who have revealed yourself to it as law when it was sliding into lawlessness;

⁶who have revealed yourself to it when it had already been vanquished by Satan,
> you who have overcome its adversary when it took refuge in you;

⁷who have given it your hand and raised it up from the clutches of Hades,
> you who have not allowed it to carry on life dictated by the body;

⁸who have shown it its very enemy,
> you who have made knowledge based upon you pure,
> O God, Lord Jesus,
> Father of supra-celestial beings, God of celestial beings,

⁹regulator of ethereal beings, guide of aerial beings,
> protector of terrestrial beings and terror of subterranean beings:
> receive the soul of your servant John, if it is indeed deemed worthy by you.

113 You who have kept me until this hour pure for yourself and unsullied by intercourse with a woman;ᵃ
²who appeared to me when I was young and wished to marry,
> saying, 'John, I need you,'

113:1–11 • This passage may be an interpolation. It suggests that male celibacy requires absolute avoidance of women. This is not characteristic of the *Acts of John*. See Appendix A.2.

you who, when I was about to wed, sent a
providential disability;
³who, when in my disobedience I planned yet a third
time to marry,
put an obstacle in my path, and later said to me,
while I was on the water at 9:00 A.M.,
'John, if you were not mine, I would have let you
marry';
⁴who blinded me for two years and gave me over to grief
and entreaty to you,
you who in the third year opened the eyes of my
mind[a]
and restored my visible eyes to me also;
⁵who, when I had regained my sight,
decreed to me how hateful it is even to fasten my
eyes upon a woman,
you who have delivered me from transitory illusion
and guided me to what abides forever;
⁶who have detached me from the foul madness inherent
in the flesh,
you who have taken from me bitter death[a] and
established me upon you alone;
⁷who have muzzled the latent diseases of my soul and
eliminated its manifest symptoms,
you who have suppressed and exiled the rebel which
lurked within me;
⁸who have made spotless my love for you,
you who have prepared for me an unbroken path to
you;
⁹who have given me undoubting faith in you,
you who have outlined for me pure knowledge of you,
¹⁰who give to all just recompense for their deeds,
you who have disposed my soul to consider no
possession more precious than you.

¹¹"Now, therefore, since I have fulfilled the assignment with
which I was entrusted by you, Lord Jesus, deem me worthy of your

113:4 [a]Cf. Eph 1:18;
APt 37:9; 39:3; ATh
28:2; 53:6; 65:6; 166:2
113:6 [a]Cf. AAnMt 2:7

113:4 • On blinding in relation to missionary commission see Acts 9.

113:10 *who give to all ...*: This phrase is probably a later addition. Cf. Ps 62:12; Prov 24:12; Mt 16:27; Rom 2:6; 2 Tim 4:14; 1 Pet 1:17; Rev 2:23; 2 Clem 1:1.

114:4 ᵃCf. Jas 2:19
115:2 ᵃ ► 110:2

rest, and grant me my final goal in you: ineffable and inexpressible salvation.

114 As I am on my way to you,
  let the fire retreat;
²let darkness be vanquished,
  let the abyss grow feeble;
³let the furnace turn cold,
  let Gehenna be quenched;
⁴let angels revere,
  let demons tremble;ᵃ
⁵let the rulers be crushed,
  let the powers fall;
¹⁰let the places on the right hand stand secure,
  let those on the left not endure;
¹¹let the Devil be muzzled,
  let Satan be derided;
¹²let his furor be extinguished,
  let his raving be calmed;
¹³let his vengeance be disgraced,
  let his assault dissolve in agony;
¹⁴let his children suffer,
  and let his entire root be banned.

¹⁵"Grant that I may complete my journey to you without injury or insult, receiving what you have promised to those who live purely and love only you."

115 After he had signed himself all over with the cross, John drew himself up and said, "Be with me, Lord Jesus Christ," and lay down in the ditch where he had spread out his garments. ²He then said, "Peace be with you,ᵃ sisters and brothers," and gave up his spirit, rejoicing.

115:1–2 • Most of this brief final chapter appears to represent a later hand.
115:2 • *gave up his spirit*: παρέδωκε τὸ πνεῦμα, as in Jn 19:30; AAnPas 63:6; cf. AcPet 40:3.

APPENDIX A

FRAGMENTARY TEXTS OF THE ACTS OF JOHN

1 OXYRHYNCHUS PAPYRUS (P. OXY.) 850

Each of these fragmentary episodes appears to be reflected also in a late medieval Irish text, the *Liber Flavus*, which allows a coherent reconstruction of the story. Zeuxis is evidently a (recent) convert who has fallen into some grave sin and is refused, or himself declines, the eucharist; he then dashes out, bent on suicide. The good deacon Verus receives the assignment of rescuing him and returning him to the assembly. As P. Oxy. 850 (verso) opens, Zeuxis is engaged in seeking John's prayers, following a public confession. The apostle then offers a prayer of thanksgiving, and, apparently, administers communion to Zeuxis alone; the others are abstaining out of fear of profanation. Noteworthy here is that in the more fully preserved sections of the *Acts of John* there is no reference to the eucharistic cup. Hence this passage may be from a more "orthodox" edition, or from an epitome.

The text appears to leap immediately into another episode, involving the proconsul and the receipt of an imperial communication, presumably dealing with a legal issue of concern to the Christians; note that a Roman governor was mentioned earlier, in AJn 31:3.

The recto includes a subheading that suggests the story about Andronikos imprisoning his wife Drusiana for denying conjugal favors; but the content does not treat these matters. John is apparently alone and on the way toward a group of believers—presumably

---

P. Oxy. 850: For editions and discussion of these fragments, see Grenfell-Hunt, *Oxyrhynchus Papyri V*, 12–18; C. Wessely, P. Oxy. 18.3 (1924) 483–85; Schäferdiek, "Acts of John," 206–8; Junod-Kaestli 1.109–36; and Spittler, *Animals* 116–24. The present translation follows the text as restored in Junod-Kaestli 1.119–22. Ellipse marks (...) give no indication of the exact length of lacunae, and the brackets give no more than an approximation as to missing and supplied spaces and characters. The Irish text is translated in Herbert and McNamara, *Apocrypha*, 91–94.

his accustomed traveling companions. A bridge is evidently mentioned: bridges were traditional habitats of demons (like those of trolls), and the soldier who menaces the apostle is, in fact, nothing other than a demon. John's reply suggests that the demon threatens him—in vain, it transpires, since the demon vanishes at John's pronouncement.

The apostle then crosses to his companions and bids them to join him in a prayer of thanksgiving. Junod-Kaestli surmise that this incident is the prelude to a miracle in which the apostle transforms straw into gold, then back into straw, as an illustration of the ephemeral character of riches. They further propose that the papyrus text, which may be dated to the fourth century CE, is a condensation of the original (*Acta Ioannis* 1. 128–29).

(Verso)
¹...] for him ... [for example, he emitted] groans and ... but John ... to [Zeux]is, ... arose and took a [cup and praye]d, ²"..., who have required me to c[hange the mind of] one intent upon hanging himself, who tu[rn] the despairing ... [for example, hearts] to you, who [al]one make known the [thoughts] know[n] to n[o] one, who weeps for the oppres[sed] ... who raises the dead ... Jesus, leader of the unempowered, advocate [for example, for the ...], ³we praise you and we venerate you an[d] we than[k you] for your every gift, especially your present dispensat[ion] and servi[ce]."

⁴Then he ad[ministered] the euchar[ist] to Zeuxis only. ⁵To those who w[is]hed to partake ... having [s]een, they did not dare.

⁶Then the Roman governo[r ...] in[to] the midst of the assem[bl]y ... s[ai]d to [John], "Servant of the unnameable ... [*a proper name is missing here*] has brought letters from Caes[ar] ... and with ..."

(Recto)
⁷...] he [*or:* she] left.

⁸Andronikos and [his wife ...]

⁹A few [days] later, [John] s[aw in a drea]m that [he was approaching] a large number of believers and passing [over] a bridge beneath which flowed a ... r[i]ver. ¹⁰As John was [dr]awing near to t[h]e believe[rs], a certain [ma]n [wear]ing a milita[ry] uniform approached him and, standing face to

P. Oxy. 850:8 [his wife]: In the photograph published in P. Oxy. VI, γυνή seems legible, but Junod-Kaestli do not accept the reading. In any case, this fragment does not mention Andronikos and Drusiana.

face, said, "John, if y[ou are he], you will soon be [in my] hand[s]."

¹¹John [replied], "The Lord will quench your threat [an]d anger, a[nd] offen[se]."

¹²And so it was: he vanished.

¹³J[o]hn then, g[oin]g on to those toward whom he was traveling, and fin[ding the]m gathered together, said, "Let us [ris]e, [my sisters and broth]ers, and bend our knees to the Lord, who has annul[led] [ev]en the [in]visible working of the gre[at enemy]." ¹⁴After he [had explai]ned ... to [th]em, he knelt down with th[em] ... [and prayed], "God. ..."

2 QUOTATIONS IN THE
PSEUDO-TITUS EPISTLE

These quotations derive from a fifth-century Spanish or Gallican exhortation known as the *Pseudo-Titus Epistle*. The subject of this homiletic material, composed in vulgar Latin, is chastity; patristic exhortations to continence often preserve quotations from NT apocrypha. Words in italics are the introductions to the quotations supplied by the author of *Pseudo-Titus*; parenthetical page and line references are to the text in de Bruyne, "Epistula Titi."

1. Quotation 1 closely resembles the opening of AJn 113. The author of the *Epistle* may have had direct access to the text or may have found it in an anthology:

> *Hear the thanksgiving of John, the disciple of the Lord, how shortly before his death he said,* "Lord, who have kept me untouched by a woman from infancy until my present age, who have kept my body so separate since then that even the sight of a woman has been hateful to me." (p. 58, ll. 436–40)

2. Quotation 2 speaks of Verus, a deacon who frequently serves as the apostle's forerunner. This and the preceding fragment, like AJn 113, represent a misogynistic position that is at variance with much of the content of the Acts, in which men and women live together in celibacy:

> *Can what we teach be beyond the demands of the law? Consider what the very demons confessed to Dyrus [= Verus] the Deacon at John's arrival:* "Many will come to us in the last days to root us out of our vessels. They will claim to be pure and unsullied by women and not burdened by sexual desire for them. But if we wished to do so, we could possess even them." (p. 59, ll. 444–49)

3. Quotation 3 reflects a setting similar to that of ATh 11–16, in which Thomas uses the occasion of a wedding reception to deliver an exhortation on sexual continence to newlyweds soon to consummate their union. (If this similarity is due to direct borrowing, the *Acts of John* is likely the more original.) See the sermon of Ælfric, under "Reception" in the Introduction. With regard to the present case, readers are evidently to understand that the homily was taken to heart and that the wedding feast came to a chaste and, from the author's point of view, a happy ending:

> *Therefore take to heart the admonitions of Saint John, who accepted an invitation to a wedding only to promote the cause of chastity. What did he say on that occasion?* "My dear children, while your flesh is still unsullied and you maintain your bodies intact and unperishing, while you have not been contaminated by Satan, who is chastity's most shameless and implacable opponent, learn more completely the secret meaning of sexual union. It is a wile of the serpent based upon ignorance of true doctrine. It damages the divine seed; it is a gift brought by and bringing death; it is the price of obliteration, the schoolroom of disunion, the reward of corruption, the [source] of boorishness; it is the seed sown by the enemy, Satan's lure, a machination of the malevolent one, the rotten fruit of human birth, the effusion of blood, a madness in the soul and a decline in the mind, a token of the fall, an instrument of punishment, a work of fire, a sign of the enemy, the noxious malice of envy, a deceiving embrace, a bitter coupling, a poison for the soul, a discovery bringing destruction, a lust for that which does not exist, a material imbroglio, an amusement of the devil, animosity toward true life, a fetter of darkness, drunkenness [of mind], an outrage of the enemy, an obstacle to authentic life that separates one from the Lord, the beginning of disobedience, the end of life, death.

"Now that you have heard this, my dear young children, unite yourselves in a genuine, sacred and indissoluble union, and look forward to the one, genuine, and incomparable consort from heaven, Christ, the eternal spouse." (p. 59, ll. 458–77)

APPENDIX B

OTHER TRADITIONS ABOUT THE APOSTLE JOHN

1 JOHN AND THE PARTRIDGE

This is an independent anecdote about the apostle John, found in one Greek manuscript (*Parisinus gr.* 1468 [Q]; there is a similar anecdote in John Cassian *Conference* 24.21). The style, form, conception, and vocabulary of this episode reveal that it was no part of the ancient *Acts of John*. In its present form it is a tract intended for the edification of clergy and religious. Its meaning derives from the common use of a bird as a symbol of the soul: Greek-readers may well have associated πέρδιξ ("partridge") with a verb of similar sound meaning "break wind" or "defecate." Junod-Kaestli 1.145–56) supply convincing reasons for not including this episode in the ancient AJn.

56 One day, while John was seated, a partridge darted down and began to roll about in the dirt before him, caking itself with its own filth. ²John gazed at it in astonishment.

³A certain priest, who was one of his listeners, approached him and saw the partridge rolling around in front of him. ⁴He took offense at this and said to himself, "Does such a person enjoy, at his age, a partridge rolling in the dust?"

⁵Then John, made aware by the Spirit of the priest's thought, replied, "It would be preferable for you, child, to watch a partridge rolling in the dust than to foul yourself with shameful and profane activities. ⁶For this is why the one who awaits the conversion and repentance of all has led you to this place. ⁷Now I have no need of a bespattered partridge: the partridge is your soul."

57 When the old man heard this, he realized that he had not gone undetected but that the apostle of Christ had told

---

56:1• This is the implication of the text, which would be strictly rendered "rolled about in the dust," as it is hereafter.

him all that was within his heart, he thrust his face to the ground and cried out: ²"Now I realize that God abides in you, blessed John, and blessed is the one who has not put God to the test through you, for whoever tempts you tempts one who cannot be tempted." ³He beseeched John to pray for him.

⁴John offered him instruction, gave him rules, sent him to his own home, and then praised the God who is over all.

2 MISCELLANEOUS TRADITIONS

1. Clement of Alexandria (*Quis dives* 42) reports a story about an encounter between John and a bandit chief. In its present form this derives from Clement, though a legend may lie behind it:

> When, on the tyrant's death, he returned to Ephesus from the isle of Patmos, he went away, being invited, to the contiguous territories of the nations, here to appoint bishops, there to set in order whole Churches, there to ordain such as were marked out by the Spirit.

2. Tertullian is the first to report the story of the apostle being thrust into a vat of boiling oil (*De praescrip.* 36.3). He may also be responsible for locating this incident in Rome:

> Since, moreover, you are close upon Italy, you have Rome, from which there comes even into our own hands the very authority (of apostles themselves). How happy is its church, on which apostles poured forth all their doctrines along with their blood! Where Peter endures a passion like his Lord's! Where Paul wins his crown in a death like John [the Baptist's]! Where the apostle John was first plunged, unhurt, into boiling oil, and thence remitted to his island-exile!

3. According to Eusebius (*Hist. eccl.* 5.18.14), the anti-Montanist author Apollonius alleged that the Montanists told a story of a resurrection performed by John at Ephesus. This could, of course, derive from the *Acts of John*.

> Furthermore, he (Apollonius) states on the authority of tradition that the Savior commanded his apostles not to leave Jerusalem for twelve years. He also makes use of evidence from the Revelation of John; and he relates how

---

Miscellaneous Traditions: • For summary judgments as to the authenticity of these stories, see Junod-Kaestli 1.156–57.

by divine power a dead man was raised by John himself in Ephesus. He makes other statements, too, by which he has ably and fully demonstrated the error of the heresy under discussion.

4. Irenaeus (*Adv. haer.* 3.3.4) tells of an encounter between John and Cerinthus in the baths at Ephesus:

> There are also those who heard from him (Polycarp) that John, the disciple of the Lord, going to bathe at Ephesus, and perceiving Cerinthus within, rushed out of the bath-house without bathing, exclaiming, "Let us fly, lest even the bath-house fall down, because Cerinthus, the enemy of the truth, is within."

APPENDIX C

OTHER NARRATIVES ABOUT THE APOSTLE JOHN

Note: With one major exception (2) these texts are of very limited value for reconstructing AJn. They show the desire for narratives about the son of Zebedee that conformed to later orthodox theology.

1. *The Syriac History of John.*[1] (CANT 215.II) Composed perhaps in the late fourth century, this work has some parallels to AJn (and *Acts of John* [by Prochorus]). It is centered in Ephesus and includes a visit in which Peter and Paul visit there to convince John that he should write a gospel.[2]

2. The aforementioned *The Acts of John by Prochorus.*[3] (CANT 218) Easily the most popular narrative about John ever written, with over 150 Greek manuscripts, the work was attributed to Prochorus, one of the Seven (Acts 6:5), who served the apostle as companion and amanuensis. Probably written in the fifth century, the text was disseminated in several languages. Roughly two-thirds of the text is situated on Patmos, the mission to which long occupied our apostle. One obstacle was the magician Cynops ("dog-face"), an avatar of the Simon Magus Peter bested in Rome (APt). Overlap with AJn may be through a secondary, bowdlerized source.

3. The *Virtutes Johannis* and the *Passio Johannis.*[4] (CANT 219–20) The former is in the collection of apostolic lives known as Pseudo-Abdias; the latter is wrongly attributed to Melitus of Laodicea. These Latin texts derive from editions of AJn. The *Virtutes* provide

---

1. Translation: Wright, 3–60; critical discussion, Junod-Kaestli 2:705–17. Culpepper, *John,* 223–30, gives a lengthy summary.

2. Peter is associated with the Gospel of Mark and Paul, less firmly, with that of Luke.

3. Text: Zahn (a new edition is desirable); no translation; Culpepper, *John,* 206–22 has a detailed summary; critical discussion: Junod-Kaestli 2:718–49.

4. For text and comment see Junod-Kaestli 2:750–814; brief summary and discussion in Culpepper, *John,* 202–4.

an accurate rendition of chapters 63–86 (Kallimachos and Drusiana) and the death scene (chapters 106–15). These or kindred sources provided The Irish and Anglo-Saxons with their knowledge of AJn.

4. The *Acts of John at Rome*.[5] (CANT 216) This Greek narrative of perhaps the fifth century fills in gaps. Taken from Ephesus to Rome John sufficiently impresses Nero to receive exile—like a VIP—to Patmos, which he leaves for Ephesus under Trajan (98–117).

---

5. Text and discussion in Junod-Kaestli 2:835–86. Translation Pick, *Apocryphal Acts*, 126–35. Culpepper, *John*, 205–6 has a useful brief discussion.

BIBLIOGRAPHY

(With occasional notes for the general reader)

EDITIONS, VERSIONS, RESEARCH AIDS

Allberry, C. R. C., ed. *A Manichaean Psalm-Book.* Vol. 2, part II. Stuttgart: W. Kohlhammer, 1938. (These poems allude to various ApocActs.)

Bonnet, Maximilian. Pp. 151-216 in vol. 2.1 of *Acta Apostolorum Apocrypha.* 2 vols in 3 books. Eds. Richard A. Lipsius and Maximilien Bonnet. Lipsiae: H. Mendelssohn, 1891-1903.

Bovon, François, Yuko Taniguchi, and Athanasios Antonopoulos. "The Memorial of Saint John the Theologian (BHG 919fb)." Pp. 333-53 in *The Apocryphal Acts of the Apostles.* Eds. F. Bovon, Ann G. Brock, C. R. Matthews. Cambridge: Harvard University Press, 1999.

Bruyne, de, D. "de 'Epistula Titi, discipuli Pauli, de disposition sanctimonii.'" *Revue Bénédictine* 37 (1925) 47-72.

Budge, E. A. Wallis. *The Contendings of the Apostles: Being the Histories and the Lives and Martyrdoms and Deaths of the Twelve Apostles and Evangelists.* 2nd ed. London: Oxford University Press, 1935, 186-220. (The Ethiopic tradition is derived from the Syriac.)

Charlesworth, James H. *The New Testament Apocrypha and Pseudepigrapha.* ATLA Bibliography Series 17. Metuchen, NJ: 1987, 229-38 (a full collection of earlier bibliography).

Corsaro, F. *Le PRAXEIS di Giovanni.* Catania: Universita di Catania Press, 1968.

Danker, Frederick W. *Jesus and the New Age: A Commentary on Luke's Gospel.* Rev. ed. Philadelphia: Fortress, 1988.

Elliott, J. Keith. *The Apocryphal New Testament: A Collection of Apocryphal Christian Literature in English Translation.* Oxford: Clarendon, 1993, 303-49. (This is the most recent collection of translations of the apocrypha in English. For introductions prefer Schneemelcher.)

Geerard, Mavrith. *Clavis Apocryphorum Novi Testamenti.* Turnhout: Brepols, 1992, §215-24. (Here one finds the data on editions and versions; a CANT number refers to this book.)

Hengel, Martin. *The Johannine Question.* Trans. J. Bowden. London: SCM, 1989.

Jakab, A. "Actes de Jean: État de la recherche (1982-1999)." *Rivista di Storia e Letteratura Religiosa* 36 (2000) 299-334.

James, Montague Rhodes. "A Fragment of the Acts of John." *Apocrypha Anecdota.* Series 2. Texts and Studies 5.1. Cambridge: Cambridge University Press, 1897, ix-xxviii. (The initial publication of AJn 87-105, with many still useful textual comments.)

Junod, Eric and Jean-Daniel Kaestli. *Acta Iohannis.* CCSA 1-2. 2 vols. Turnhout: Brepols, 1983. (This is the standard critical edition.)

———. "Actes de Jean." Pp. 975-1037 in *Écrits apocryphes chrétiens.* Eds. F. Bovon and Pierre Geoltrain. 2 vols. Paris: Gallimard, 1997.

———. "Le dossier des 'Actes de Jean.'" *Aufstieg und Niedergang der römischen Welt: Geschichte und Kultur Roms im Spiegel der neueren Forschung* (ANRW) 2.25.6 (1988) esp. 4357-62.

Leloir, Louis. *Écrits apocryphes sur les apôtres: Traduction de l'édition arménienne de Venise*. Vol. 1. CCSA 3 Turnhout: Brepols, 1986.
Máire, Herbert and Martin McNamara. *Irish Biblical Apocrypha: Selected Texts in Translation*. London: T&T Clark, 2004.
Pick, Bernard. *The Apocryphal Acts*. Chicago: Open Court, 1909, 126-95.
Schäferdiek, Knut. "The Acts of John." Pp. 152-71 in vol. 2 of *New Testament Apocrypha*. Ed. Wilhelm Schneemelcher. (Schneemelcher is the best general introduction to the Apocrypha.)
Wright, William. *Apocryphal Acts of the Apostles. Edited from Syriac Manuscripts in the British Museum and Other Libraries*. 2 vols. London: Williams and Norgate, 1871, 2:3-68.
Zahn, Theodor. *Acta Ioannis unter Benutzung von C. Tischendorf's Nachlass bearbeitet*. Erlangen: Deichert, 1880. (This is the *Acts of John* by Prochorus, a late work that incorporates much of the ancient AJn, perhaps indirectly.)

STUDIES

Adamik, T. "The influence of the apocryphal Acts on Jerome's Lives of Saints." Pp. 171-82 in *The Apocryphal Acts of John*. Ed. Jan. N. Bremmer.
Böhlig, A. "Zur Vorstellung vom Lichtkreuz in Gnostizimus und Manichäismus." Pp. 473-91 in *Gnosis*. Hans Jonas FS. Göttingen: Vandenhoeck & Ruprecht, 1978.
Bolyki, J. "Miracle Stories in the Acts of John." Pp. 15-35 in *The Apocryphal Acts of John*. Ed. Jan. N. Bremmer.
Bowe, B. E. "Dancing into the Divine: The Hymn of the Dance in the Acts of John." *Journal of Early Christian Studies* 7 (1999) 83-84.
Breckenridge, J. D. "Apocrypha of Early Christian Portraiture." *Byzantinische Zeitschrift* 67 (1974) 101-9.
Bremmer, Jan N., ed. *The Apocryphal Acts of John*. SAAA 1. Kampen: Kok Pharos, 1995.
———. "Women in the Apocryphal Acts of John." Pp. 37-56 in *The Apocryphal Acts of John*.
Bremmer, R. H. "The reception of the Acts of John in AngloSaxon England." Pp. 183-96 in *The Apocryphal Acts of John*. Ed. Jan. N. Bremmer.
Brioso, M. "Sobre el 'Tanzhymnus' de Acta Ioannis 94-96." *Emerita* 40 (1972) 31-45.
Brown, Phyllis R., ed. *A Companion to Hrotsvit of Gandersheim*. Leiden: Brill, 2012.
Brown, Raymond E. *The Epistles of John*. Anchor Bible Commentaries 30; Garden City, NY: Doubleday, 1982.
Cartlidge, David R. "Evangelist Leaves Wife, Clings to Christ: An Illustration in the Admont 'Anselm' and its Relevance to a Reconstruction of the *Acta Iohannis*." Pp. 376-89 in *Society of Biblical Literature Seminar Papers* (SBLSP) 1994. Atlanta: Scholars, 1994.
——— and J. Keith Elliott. *Art and the Christian Apocrypha*. London: Routledge, 2001.
Culpepper, R. Alan. *John, the Son of Zebedee*. Minneapolis: Fortress, 2000. (This discusses the legend of John from ancient to modern times, including apocryphal traditions. Pp. 187-250 survey AJn and related traditions.)
Czachesz, István. *Commission Narratives: A Comparative Study of the Canonical and Apocryphal Acts*. Studies on Early Christian Apocrypha 8. Leuven: Peeters, 2007.
———. "Early Christian Views on Jesus' Resurrection: Toward a Cognitive Psychological Interpretation." *Nederlands Theologisch Tijdschrift* 61(1) (2007) 47-59.

———. "Eroticism and Epistemology in the Apocryphal Acts of John." *Nederlands Theologisch Tijdschrift* 60 (2006) 59–72.

———. "The Gospel of the Acts of John: Its Relation to the Fourth Gospel." Pp. 49–72 in *The Legacy of John*. Ed. Rasimus Tuomus. SupNovT 132. Leiden: Brill, 2009.

———. "The Grotesque Body in Early Christian Discourse: Hell, Scatology, and Metamorphosis." Pp. 115-29 in *BibleWorld*. Sheffield: Equinox, 2012.

Dewey, Arthur J. "The Hymn in *The Acts of John*: Dance as Hermeneutic." *Semeia* 38 (1986) 67–80 (and a response by J.-D. Kaestli, 81–88).

Elliott, Alison Goddard. *Roads to Paradise: Reading the Lives of the Early Saints*. Hanover, NH: The University Press of New England, 1987. (A guide to the use of fiction in hagiography.)

Engelmann, Helmut. "Ephesos und die Johannesakten." *Zeitschrift für Papyrologie und Epigraphik (ZPE)* 103 (1994) 297–302.

Findlay, Adam F. *Byways in Early Christian Literature: Studies in the Uncanonical Gospels and Acts*. Edinburgh: T&T Clark, 1923.

Garcia, H. "La polymorphie du Christ. Remarques sur quelques definitions et sur des multiples enjeux." *Apocrypha* 10 (1999) 16–55.

Gardner, I. and K. Worp. "Leaves from a Manichaean Codex." *Zeitschrift für Papyrologie und Epigraphik (ZPE)* 117 (1997) 139–55. (See Jenkins, of which this is a new edition.)

Hennecke, E. and G. Schimmelpfeng. *Handbuch zu den Neutestamentlichen Apokryphen*. Tübingen: Mohr, 1904, 492–543.

Herceg, P. "The Sermons of the Book of Acts and the Apocryphal Acts." Pp. 153–70 in *The Apocryphal Acts of John*. Ed. Jan. N. Bremmer.

Herbert, Maire and Martin McNamara. *Irish Biblical Apocrypha*. London: Bloomsbury T&T Clark, 2004.

Jenkins, G. "Papyrus 1 from Kellis. A Greek text with affinities to the Acts of John." Pp. 197–229 in *The Apocryphal Acts of John*. Ed. Jan. N. Bremmer. (See Gardner, who has reedited this material.)

Jones, F. Stanley. "Principal Orientations on the Relations between the Apocryphal Acts (*Acts of Paul* and *Acts of John; Acts of Peter* and *Acts of John*)." Pp. 485–505 in *Society of Biblical Literature Seminar Papers* 1993. Atlanta: Scholars, 1993.

Junod, Eric and Jean-Daniel Katestli. *L'histoire des actes apocryphes des apôtres du IIIe au IXe siècle*. CRThPh 7. Lausanne: Faculté de theologie, 1982.

———. "Le dossier des 'Actes de Jean': état de la question et perspectives nouvelles." Pp. 4293–4362 in *Aufstieg und Niedergang der römischen Welt* (ANRW) 25.6. Ed. Wolfgang Haase. Berlin: de Gruyter, 1988.

———. "Le role des textes bibliques dans la gènese et le développement des legends apocryphes: Le cas du sort final de l'apôtre Jean." *Augustinianum (Aug)* 23 (1983) 319–36.

———. "Les traits caractéristiques de la théologie des 'Actes de Jean.'" *Revue de théologie et de philosophie* 26 (1976) 125–45.

Kaestli, Jean-Daniel. "Le mystère de la crois de lumière et le Johannisme. Actes de Jean ch. 94-102." *Foi et vie 86 (Cahier biblique 26)* (1987) 35–46.

———. "Les Scènes d'attribution des champs de mission et de depart de l'apôtres dans les actes aocryphes." Pp. 249–64 in *Les Actes Apocryphes des Apôtres: christianisme et monde païen*. François Bovon et al. Geneva: Labor et Fides, 1981.

Karasszon, I. "Old Testament quotations in the Acts of Andrew and John." Pp. 57-71 in *The Apocryphal Acts of John*. Ed. Jan N. Bremmer.

Käsemann, Ernst. *The Testament of Jesus*. Trans. Gerhard Krodel. Philadelphia: Fortress, 1968.

Klauck, Hans-Joseph. *The Apocryphal Acts of the Apostles: An Introduction*. Trans. Brian McNeil. Waco, TX: Baylor University Press, 2008, 15-45. (This is the best handbook on the subject.)

———. "Christus in vielen Gestalten: Die Polymorphie des Erlösers in apokryphen Texten." Pp. 303-74 in Klauck, *Die apokryphe Bibel*. Tübingen: Mohr Siebek, 2008.

Koester, Helmut. "Ephesos in Early Christian Literature." Pp. 119-40 in *Ephesos: Metropolis of Asia: An Interdisciplinary Approach to its Archaeology, Religion, and Culture*. Ed. Helmut Koester. Harvard Theological Studies 41. Valley Forge: Trinity, 1995.

Konstan, David. "Acts of Love: A Narrative Pattern in the Apocryphal Acts." *Journal of Early Christian Studies* 6 (1998) 15-36.

Lallemann, Pieter J. *The Acts of John: A Two Stage Initiation into Johannine Gnosticism*. SAAA 4. Leuven: Peeters, 1982.

———. "Polymorphy of Christ." Pp. 97-118 in *The Apocryphal Acts of John*. Ed. Jan. N. Bremmer.

Limberis, Vasiliki. "The Council of Ephesos: The Demise of the See of Ephesos and the Rise of the Cult of the Theotokos." Pp. 321-40 in *Ephesos: Metropolis of Asia: An Interdisciplinary Approach to its Archaeology, Religion, and Culture*. Ed. Helmut Koester. Harvard Theological Studies (HTS) 41. Valley Forge: Trinity, 1995.

Lipsius, Richard A. *Die apokryphen Apostelgeschichten*. Vol. 1 repr. of 1883. Amsterdam: Philo, 1976, 348-542.

Luttikhuizen, G. "A gnostic reading of the Acts of John." Pp. 119-52 in *The Apocryphal Acts of John*. Ed. Jan N. Bremmer.

MacDonald, Dennis R. "Jesus and Dionysian Polymorphism in the *Acts of John*." Pp. 97-104 in *Early Jewish and Christian Narrative: The Role of Religion in Shaping Narrative Forms*. Eds. I Ramelli and J. Perkins. Tübingen: Mohr Siebeck, 2015.

———. "Which Came First? Intertextual Relationships among the Apocryphal Acts of the Apostles." *Semeia* 80 (1997) 11-41.

———. "Who Was that Chaste Prostitute? A Socratic Answer to an Enigma in the *Acts of John*." Pp. 88-97 in *A Feminist Companion to the New Testament Apocrypha*. Ed. Amy-Jill Levine. London: T&T Clark, 2006.

MacNamara, Martin. *The Apocrypha in the Irish Church*. Dublin: Institute for Advanced Studies, 1975.

———. *The Bible and the Apocrypha in the Early Irish Church 600-1200 A.D.* Turnhout: Brepols, 2015.

Nogueira, Paulo. "Powerful public performances and literary subversion of social reality in the Early Christianity: the case of the Apostle John in the Artemision (Acts of John 37-47)." Unpublished paper delivered at Ancient Fiction and Early Jewish and Christian Narrative Section, San Diego, CA, November 2014.

Painchaud, Louis. *Le deuxième traité du grand Seth NH VII, 2*. BCNH 6. Québec: les Presses de l'université Laval, 1982.

Perkins, Judith. *Roman Imperial Identities in the Early Christian Era*. London: Routledge, 2009.

Pervo, Richard I. "Acts." In *Oxford Handbook to the Christian Apocrypha*. Eds. A. Gregory and C. Tuckett (forthcoming 2015).

———. *Acts. A Commentary.* Ed. H. W. Attridge. Hermeneia. Minneapolis: Fortress, 2009.

———. *The Acts of Paul: A New Translation with Introduction and Commentary.* Salem, Oregon: Cascade, 2014.

———. "Apostles." In *Oxford Handbook to the Christian Apocrypha*. Eds. A. Gregory and C. Tuckett (forthcoming 2015).

———. "Egging on the Chickens: A Cowardly Response to Dennis MacDonald and Then Some." *Semeia* 80 (1997) 43–56.

———. "Johannine Trajectories in the Acts of John." *Apocrypha* 3 (1992) 47–68.

———. *The Making of Paul: Constructions of the Apostle in Early Christianity.* Minneapolis: Fortress, 2010.

———. *Profit with Delight: The Literary Genre of the Acts of the Apostles.* Philadelphia: Fortress, 1987.

———. "Rhetoric in the Christian Apocrypha," Pp. 793–805 in *A Handbook of Classical Rhetoric in the Hellenistic Period 330 B.C.–A.D. 400*. Ed. S. Porter. Leiden: Brill, 1998.

Plümacher, Eckhard. "Apostolische Missionsreise und statthalterliche Assisetour. Eine Interpretation von Acta Johanis c. 37–45 und 55." *Zeitschrift für die neutestamentliche Wissenschaft und die Kunde der älteren Kirche* 85 (1994) 259–78 (= *Geschichte und Geschichten*, 207–28).

———. *Geschichte und Geschichten: Aufsätze zur Apostelgeschichte und zu den Johannesakten.* WUNT 170. Tübingen: Mohr Siebeck, 2004.

———. "Der ἄφθονος θεός in Acta Johannis 55 und sein historischer Kontext." Pp. 229–73 in *Geschichte und Geschichten*.

———. "Paignion und Biberfabel: zum literarischen und popularphilosophischen Hintergrund von Acta Iohannis 60 f.48–54." *Apocrypha* 3 (1992) 69–109 (= *Geschichte und Geschichten*, 171–206).

Robinson, James M. "Jesus: From Easter to Valentinus (or to the Apostles' Creed)." *Journal of Biblical Literature* (*JBL*) 101 (1982) 5–37.

———, general editor. *The Nag Hammadi Library in English.* Rev. ed.; San Francisco: Harper & Row, 1988.

———. and Helmut Koester. *Trajectories through Early Christianity.* Philadelphia: Fortress, 1971.

Roldanus, H. "Die Eucharistie in den Johannes-Akten." Pp. 72–96 in *The Apocryphal Acts of John*. Ed. Jan N. Bremmer.

Rose, Els. *Ritual Memory: The Apocryphal Acts and Liturgical Commemoration in the Early Medieval West (c. 500–1215).* Leiden: Brill, 2009.

Santos Otero, Aurelio. "Later Acts of Apostles." Pp. 429–36 in vol. 2 of *New Testament Apocrypha*. Ed. Wilhelm Schneemelcher.

Sirker-Wicklaus, Gerlinde. *Untersuchungen zu den Johannes-Akten.* B R 2. Witterschlick: Wohle, 1988.

Schäferdiek, Knut. "Herkunft und Interesse der alten Johannesakten." *Zeitschrift für die neutestamentliche Wissenschaft und die Kunde der älteren Kirche* (ZNW) 74 (1983) 247–67.

———. "Johannes-Akten." *Reallexikon für Antike und Christentum* (RAC) 139–40 (1997) 564–95.

Schneemelcher, Wilhelm, ed. *New Testament Apocrypha.* 2 vols. Trans. ed. R. McL. Wilson. Louisville, KY: Westminster/John Knox, 1991–1992.

Schneider, Paul G. "The *Acts of John:* The Gnostic Transformation of a Christian Community." Pp. 241–69 in *Hellenization Revisited: Shaping a Christian Response within the Greco-Roman World*. Ed. Wendy E. Hellerman. Lanham: MD: University Press of America, 1994.

———. *The Mystery of the Acts of John*. Lewiston, NY: Mellen, 1991.

———. "A Perfect Fit: The Major Interpolation in the Acts of John." Pp. 518–32 in *Society of Biblical Literature (SBL) 1991 Seminar Papers*. Atlanta: Scholars, 1991.

Seonghee Chae. *Women's Ascetic Communities in the Acts of John*. Diss., Union Seminary. Richmond, Virginia, 2006.

Snyder, Glenn E. *Acts of Paul: The Formation of a Pauline Corpus*. Wissenschaftliche Untersuchungen zum Neuen Testament (WUNT) 352. Tübingen: Mohr Siebeck, 2013.

Snyder, Julia A. "Imitation of 'We' Passages in Acts? Canonical Influence and the Internal (First Person) Narrator of the *Acts of John"* (*JECS* forthcoming).

———. *Language and Identity in Ancient Narratives: The Relationship between Speech Patterns and Social Context in the Acts of the Apostles*, the Acts of John, *and the* Acts of Phillip. WUNT 370. Tübingen: Mohr Siebeck, 2014.

———. "Relationships between the Acts of the Apostles and Other Apostle Narratives." In *Between Canonical and Apocryphal Texts: Processes of Reception, Rewriting and Interpretation in Early Judaism and Early Christianity*. Eds. Jörg Frey, Claire Clivaz, and Tobias Nicklas. WUNT. Tübingen: Mohr Siebeck, 2015 (forthcoming).

Söder, Rosa. *Die apokryphen Apostelgeschichten und die romanhafte Literatur der Antike*. W. Kohlhammer: Stuttgart, 1932.

Spittler, Janet, E. *Animals in the Apocryphal Acts of the Apostles*. WUNT 247. Tübingen, Mohr Siebeck, 2008.

Stoops Jr., Robert F. *The Acts of Peter*. Salem, Oregon: Polebridge, 2012.

———. "The *Acts of Peter* in Intertextual Context." *Semeia* 80 (1997) 57–86.

———, ed. *Semeia* 80: *The Apocryphal Acts of the Apostles in Intertextual Perspectives* (1980).

Stroumsa, Guy H. "Christ's Laughter: Docetic Origins Reconsidered." *Journal of Early Christian Studies* (*JECS*) 12 (2004) 267–88.

Thompson, Trevor. "Claiming Ephesus: Pauline Legacy in *the Acts of John*." Pp. 379–400 in *The Rise and Expansion of Christianity in the First Three Centuries of the Common Era*. Eds. Clare K. Rothschild and Jens Schröter. WUNT 301. Tübingen: Mohr Siebeck, 2013.

Trebilco, Paul R. *The Early Christians in Ephesus from Paul to Ignatius*. WUNT 166; Tübingen: Mohr Siebeck, 2004.

Turner, E. G. *Greek Manuscripts of the Ancient World*. Princeton: Princeton University Press, 1971.

Vielhauer, Philipp. *Geschichte der urchristlichen Literatur*. Berlin: de Gruyter, 1975, 706–10.

Von Wahlde, Urban C. The *Gospel and Letters of John*. 3 vols. Grand Rapids: Eerdmans, 2010.

———. *The Johannine Commandments: 1 John and the Struggle for the Johannine Tradition*. Mahwah, NJ: Paulist, 1990.

INDEX OF ANCIENT SOURCES

1 Corinthians	
2:16	45 n.
3:1–2	52
3:16–17	42
5:4	31
4:19	32
7:9	12
11:2	48
15:3	48
15:5	38 n.
15:24	46

1 John	
	18

1 Kings	
18:17–40	50 n.

1 Peter	
1:17	77

1 Thessalonians	
3:6	31

1 Timothy	
1:17	51
6:7	37

2 Clement	
1:1	77
19:1	51

2 Corinthians	
2:17	35
6:16	42

2 Peter	
1	20 n.104

2 Timothy	
1:16	30
4:14	77 n.

4 Maccabees	
8:19	38 n.

Acts	
1:2	47
1:6	41
1:15–26	4 n.2
1:16	38
1:23	48
2:5	4 n.24
2:11	49 n.
2:14	35 n.
2:29	38
2:38	31
2:37	38
3:6	30
3:12	35 n.
3:20	30 n.
4:10	31
7:2	38
8:10	35 n.
9	5, 77 n.
10:26	32 n.
10:38	31
13:15	38
13:26	38
13:38	38
14:15	51 n.
15:7	38
15:13	38
16:18	31
17:22	35 n.
19:9	59 n.
19:20–20:1	6
19:35	35 n.
20:7–12	75 n.
22	5
22:1	38
23:1	38
23:6	38
26	5
28:17	38

Acts of Andrew
22

Acts of Andrew Passion
13:2	72
21:4	71
40:2	71
49:3	54
63:6	78

Acts of Andrew and Matthias
2:7	77
3:5	75
4:8	75

Acts of John at Rome
88

Acts of the Second Council of Nicea
3 n.15

Acts of Paul
2, n.10, 5, 8, 13 n.69, 16, 19 n.98

3:7	45 n.
4:15	70 n.
9	14 n.75
9.20	38
13:7–11	12 n.61

Acts of Peter
8, 13, 13 n.72, 16, 16 n.83

5:27	38
20	12 n.61
20:12	38
21:13	39
29:4	72
30:1	72
37:9	77
39:3	77

Acts of Thomas
4, 4, n.23, 8, 9, n.48

1:2	59
3:1	28
9:5	28 n.
12:3	36
20:7	34
27:2	75
27:3	45 n.
27:11	38
28:2	77
29:4	72
29:5	53 n.
30–41; 68–81	59 n.
30:3	53
31:1	64
31:9	72
33:2	54 n.
36:15	34
37:2	49
44:1	54 n.
44:4	30
53	38
53:6	77
53:8	30 n.
62–64	58
62:4	29
65:6	77
70:4	75
74:4	54 n.
95:8	30
100:4	47
141:6	29 n.
143:8	39
144:9	76
156:3	30
166:2	77

Aelfric
Sermon on St. John's Day
22

Aeschylus
Sept. c. Theb.
662   29 n.

Apocryphon of John
See *Secret Book of John.*

Augustine of Hippo
Epistles
237   3
Sermons
9   46

Bel et Draco
See Daniel.

Index of Ancient Sources

Chariton, *Callirhoe*
9 n.53

Clement of Alexandria
Excerpts from Theodotus
26.3   46 n.
Quis dives
42   84
Stromateis/ta
5.14   41 n.
6.5   33 n.
7.14   33 n.

Colossians
1:15–20   73
2:10   46
2:15   46
3:17   31

Daniel
7:9   39 n.
14:1–22 (=Bel et Draco)

Dio of Prusa
Or. 12   32 n.

Ecclesiastes
5:15   37 n.

Ephesians
1:18   77
1:21   48
1:22   32
1:24   46
5:26   70
6:11   56 n.
6:12   46

Epiphanius
Panarion
47.1   8 n.46
79.5   8 n.46

Epistle of the Apostles
11:8   41 n.
17:4   46 n.

Eusebius
Ecclesiastical History
3.25.6   8 n.46

5.18.14   84
6.8.2   55

Exodus
8:15 (11)   30
33:23   39 n.

Galatians
2:8   14 n.77, 75
2:9   48
2:14   33 n.

Genesis
1–3   12

Gospel of the Savior
              13 n.67

Gospel of Peter
              13 n.67
19   47

Hebrews
3:6   42
5:7   67
11:8   32

Hesiod
Theog.
902   29 n.

Homer
Iliad
13.68–72   41n.

Hrotsvitha of Gandersheim
Calimachus 22

Ignatius
Smyrnaeans
3.2   41 n.

Irenaeus
Adv. haer.
3.3.4   85

Isaiah
1:18   39
28:12   30 n.
32:15   30 n.

James
1:13	40
1:17	42
2:19	78

Job
1:21	37 n.

John
	10 n.55, 53 n.
1:1	45 n.
1:5	42
1:14	45 n.
1:17	45 n
1:40–42	38
2:1-12	22
4:35	52 n.
6:1–15	20 n.95
6:35–48	45 n.
8:44	71
9:3	28
10:7	43
10:9	43, 45 n.
10:22	49
10:30	46 n.
10:38	46 n.
11:25	45 n.
11:42	31
13:23	25, 39
13–19	21
13–20	20
13:12–17	19 n.96
14:2	42
14:6	45 n.
14:11	46 n.
16:32	45
17:21	46 n.
18:12	41
18:15	52
18:36	41
19:25–27	16 n.84
19:29	45
19:34b	21, 45, 47
20:2	39
20:11–18	17
20:19, 21, 26,	75
20:27	40
21	21
21:25	38

Luke
	10, 13, 19, 19 nn.96 & 97
1:63	28
2:29	28
5:1–11	20 n.105
6:47–49	52 n.
7:32	42
7:36	40
8:5	45 n.
8:11	45 n.
9:18–19	46
9:28–36	39
9:58	42
9:60	32, 52
11:2	28
11:9	30 n.
14:21	32
16:19–35	36
22:24–27	19
22:54	41
23:44	45
24:13–35	17
24:34	38 n.
24:39	41 n.

Manichaean Psalter
	8, 58

Mark
	9
1:16–20	38
2:1–12	10 n.57
4:46	45 n.
5:1–20	10 n.57
6:45–52	17
8:27–28	46
9:1–8	17
9:2–9	39
9:43	37
10:42–44	19
10:52	59 n.
12:13–17	10 n.56
14:26	41 n.
14:48	41
14:50	45
15:36	45
15:43	45

Index of Ancient Sources

(Pseudo-)Mark
16:19   47

Matthew
           3, 13
4:18–22   28
6:10   28
6:19   36
7:7   30 n.
7:24–27   52 n.
8:20   42
8:22   32, 52
10:28   48
11:17   42
11:28   44
13–14   46
16:27   77 n.
17:1–8   39
19:22   55 n.
26:30   41 n.
26:42   28
26:56   45
27:34   45
27:45   45
27:48   45
27:55   41
28:3   39 n.

"Nicephorus," *Stichometry*
           3, 3 n.17

Odes of Solomon
13.1   43 n.

Origen
Contra Celsum
3.15   32 n.
Schol. in Cant.
4.5   30 n.

Ovid
Fasti
3.701–4   45 n.

Oxyrhynchus Papyri
850   45, 37, 48, 79–81

Passio Johannis
           87

Philippians
2:24   32

Philostratus
Heroicus
13.2   41 n.

Plato
Symposium   5 n.32

Plotinus
Enneads
6.9.8   42 n.

Porphry
Life of Plotinus
1   32 n.

Proverbs
24:12   77 n.

Psalms
51:7   39
62:12   77 n.

Pseudo-Prochorus' *Acts of John*
           4, 87

Pseudo-Titus Epistle
           5, 27, 58, 81–82

Revelation
1:10   72
1:14   39
2:23   77 n.
2–3   5, 6

Romans
2:6   77 n.
11:13   28 n.

Sallust
           9, n.49

Second Treatise of the Great Seth
2:55   30–56, 19, 45 n.

Secret Book of John
           13

Syriac History of John
87

Tacitus
9, n.49

Tertullian
De praescrip.
36.3   84

Titus
2:7   56
3:5   70

Virtutes Johannis
87

Wisdom
7:13   56
15:3   74

ABOUT THE AUTHORS

Richard I. Pervo earned a Th.D. at Harvard University and taught religion at Seabury-Western Theological Seminary and at the University of Minnesota in Minneapolis. A Lucan specialist, he is the author of many books including *The Gospel of Luke* (Scholars Bible, 2014), *Acts of Paul: A New Translation and Commentary* (2014), *Acts: A Commentary* (Hermeneia, 2009), *The Mystery of Acts* (2008), and *Dating Acts* (2006).

Julian V. Hills (Th.D. Harvard University) is Associate Professor of Theology at Marquette University in Milwaukee, Wisconsin where he specializes in New Testament studies, with emphasis on the Johannine tradition. A recipient of the 1999 Père Marquette faculty teaching award, Hills is the series editor of the Early Christian Apocrypha and author of the ECA volume, *The Epistle of the Apostles* (2009).

www.ingramcontent.com/pod-product-compliance
Lightning Source LLC
Chambersburg PA
CBHW070934160426
43193CB00011B/1680